Tanks and Other Armoured Fighting Vehicles
1942–45

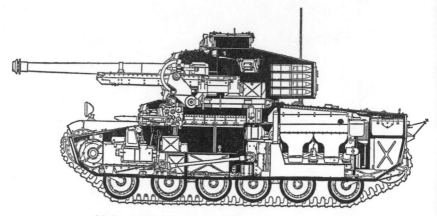

Medium Tank, Type 3 (Chi-Nu), Japan — length (hull) 18′6″

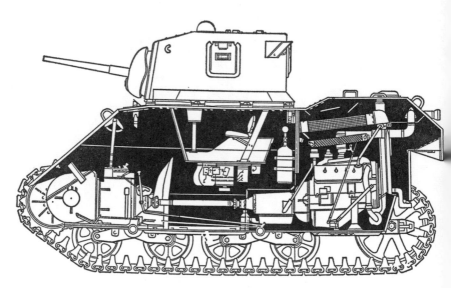

Light Tank, M.5, U.S.A. — length 14′ 2¾″

Mechanised Warfare in Colour

TANKS

and other
Armoured Fighting Vehicles
1942–45

by
B. T. WHITE

illustrated by
JOHN W. WOOD

B. Hiley
J. Pelling
E. Bruce

BLANDFORD PRESS

POOLE   DORSET

Blandford Press Ltd
Link House, West Street,
Poole, Dorset BH15 1LL

First published 1975
© Blandford Press 1975

Text and Colour printed in Great Britain by
Cox & Wyman Ltd, Fakenham, Norfolk

0 7137 0705 4

PREFACE

The period covered by this book is 1942-45, but some tanks and armoured vehicles (notably Japanese and American) developed before this have been included in order that a comparison can be made between them and late vehicles with which they were in combat or served alongside.

The wide variety of armoured vehicles of all kinds appertaining to the period has made it necessary, in many cases, to show illustrations of two different types on one page in order to increase the coverage of representative vehicles. This, in turn, has increased the difficulty of arranging the vehicles in a strict chronological order, even were it possible to reach a satisfactory decision between the relative importance of date of prototype, date of entry into production, date of entry into service, first time in action and so on. Therefore, it has been decided, for this volume, to group vehicles under countries and sub-divided into types—light tanks, medium tanks, heavy tanks, self-propelled guns, special armour, and armoured cars, in approximate chronology, where appropriate, for each type. The sequence of countries follows no particular pattern except that as several Japanese vehicles dating from before 1942 are included, the section on Japan comes first. Commonwealth A.F.V.s are mixed in with corresponding U.K. vehicles, as production and design in the Commonwealth was so closely linked with the U.K. during this period. Specialized armoured vehicles devised and built by the United Kingdom but using American chassis are listed under 'United Kingdom', although the origin of the basic vehicle is given in the text.

Camouflage colours and vehicle markings applicable to the period covered have been shown as accurately as possible on the strength of the information obtainable. However, readers particularly interested in this subject are referred to the notes in the appendix at the back of this book

Although detailed technical information cannot be provided in a small book of this kind, cross-section side elevations of representative armoured fighting vehicles of several countries are included at the back of this book to give some idea of the internal layout of the various components. Also, to supplement details mentioned in the main text, data tables for some of the leading A.F.V.s are given as an appendix.

Many printed sources, too numerous to acknowledge individually, have been used in the preparation of this book, but two small journals, published for modellers of A.F.V.s but containing the results of a great deal of original work on A.F.V. history deserve special mention—these are *Tankette* (Editor, J. P. Wilkes, 26 Stirling Grove, Whitefield, Manchester, Lancs, M25 6BY, England) and *A.F.V.News* (Editor, George Bradford, R.R. No. 2, Preston, Ontario, Canada).

The author also wishes to thank all the firms, institutions and individuals, including many friends, who have contributed over many years to his general background of knowledge of the subject. In particular, however, should be mentioned Colonel Robert J. Icks (who has an incomparable private collection on the subject of A.F.V.s), Colonel Peter Hordern, Director of the Royal Armoured Corps Tank Museum, Bovington, Dorset, England (where a fine display of A.F.V.s is open to the public) and his predecessors, and the staff of the reference departments of the Imperial War Museum, London.

Finally, for their invaluable help in converting my illegible manuscripts into typescripts, thanks are due to Mrs Betty Scotland and to Janis, my wife.

B. T. WHITE
London, 1975

INTRODUCTION

The war on land 1942–45
The beginning of 1942 was marked by notable success for Japanese arms, following the attack on the United States fleet in Pearl Harbor in December 1941 and the invasion of British, Dutch, French and U.S. overseas territories. The whole area was largely unsuited to the use of armour but, its use nevertheless, was more important than is generally supposed.

Unlike the Far East battles, armour had played the main part in the North African campaign where in April 1942 Axis forces were at the gateway to Cairo; fortunes changed at El Alamein in October and led to the Germans and Italians being expelled from the African continent, the final actions taking place in Tunisia in early 1943, where the British Eighth Army met up with the Anglo-American force that had landed in Morocco and Algeria in November of the previous year. The Mediterranean battles were transferred next to Sicily and then to Italy; much more difficult terrain for the employment of armour.

The great German–Soviet battles on the Eastern Front continued, but the halting of the Germans at Stalingrad in the winter months of 1942 was the turning point. The greatest tank battle of all time took place at Kursk in summer 1943, leading eventually to the Russians fighting their way into Berlin in April 1945.

In the West, the Anglo-Canadian raid on Dieppe in August 1942 showed the need for adequate preparations (including the development of special armoured vehicles) for the full scale invasion of North West Europe so that, despite Russian demands, D-Day did not take place until June 1944

The land war in the Far East was gradually won by the Allies (before its abrupt termination by the atomic bombs dropped on Japan itself) by the 1944–45 campaign in Burma and the island-hopping amphibious operations in the Pacific.

Armour Developments
The influence of the excellent Soviet medium and heavy tanks and the powerful German tanks developed to counter them was the predominant feature of tank development in 1942 and continued to be so for the greater part of the war. Although the later German tanks—exemplified by the Tiger I, Panther and Tiger II tended to have a slightly better armament/armour combination, the Russian tanks were the more reliable, thanks in part to the longer development history of their excellent diesel engines and, no doubt, to their less complex design. The German PzKpfw III and IV, although greatly improved, were continued in production longer than was desirable, but an earlier change to the new Panther would have left a dangerous shortage of medium tanks at a critical time. Production difficulties also led to the increased emphasis on the well-armed and armoured Sturmgeschütz at the expense of tanks. The turretless Sturmgeschütz was simpler to make but less flexible in use than a tank. An unwanted diversion from German battle-tank production was brought

about by the need for anti-aircraft tanks due to Allied air superiority. By contrast, A.A. tanks were largely dropped from British and United States formations after 1944.

British-built tanks were generally out-gunned by German armour to the end of the war, the Comet of 1944 probably being the best all-round answer to enemy medium tanks. The Cromwell was a good fast tank for reconnaissance purposes and the Churchill series were well armoured although both types were under-gunned. The Challenger (built in small numbers) and the British-modified Sherman Firefly, both with the British 17-pr gun, were for a long time the only Allied tanks on the Western front up to tackling the Tiger at all ranges. The U.S. Pershing, equal to the Tiger, arrived in small numbers only in 1945.

The American Sherman and the Russian T-34 were the outstanding tanks of the war on the Allied side. The Sherman, reliable, easy to maintain, and capable of being up-gunned from the original 75-mm. formed the main-stay of American and British armoured formations on many fronts.

Italian armour development during the period under review in essence amounted to the M.15/42 medium, developed from the closely similar M.13/40, and a switch to the produc-tion of the Semoventi. These were well-armoured self-propelled mount-ings, akin to the German Sturmge-schütz and produced to a policy similar to that of the Germans. The only Italian heavy tank was built in small quantities before the Italian armistice.

Japanese tanks were mechanically sound and were the result of a carefully thought out development plan. The lightest tanks ('tankettes') were in-tended only as infantry carriers and the light and medium tanks were no match for their Allied counterparts. The later better-armed Japanese medium tanks were built in such small numbers as to have no influence on the war. The lack of effective opposition made it possible for the British forces in Burma in 1944–45 to make good use of American-built Lee/Grant tanks, which had made their mark in the 1942 Desert campaigns but were no longer suitable for employ-ment against the Germans.

The most outstanding British contri-bution to armour in World War II was perhaps in the design and develop-ment of specialized armour, such as anti-mine flail tanks, flamethrowers, bridging tanks, armoured searchlight tanks, engineer tanks and amphibious devices. The Japanese also showed ingenuity in producing specialized armour, although apart from amphi-bians they appear to have made rela-tively little use of it. The Pacific island battles saw wide use of American tracked landing vehicles in assault, cargo and troop-carrying roles. L.V.T.s were employed by the Allies also in Italy and in major river crossings in Germany.

Self-propelled guns were used in wide variety by Germany, often as a means of putting to good use obsolescent tank chassis to give mobility to field and anti-tank weapons. Lightly armoured compared with the Sturm-geschütz type of vehicle, these self-propelled guns gave good service, despite the logistic problem the many

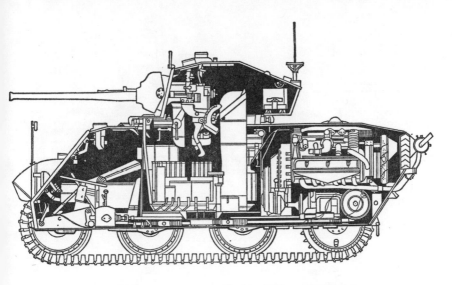

Tank, Light, Mark VIII, Harry Hopkins, U.K. — length 14′3″

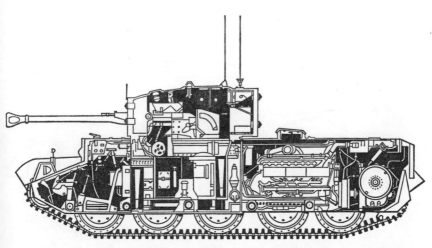

Tank, Cruiser, Cromwell VIII, U.K. — length 20′10″

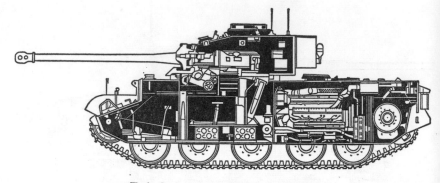

Tank, Cruiser, Comet, U.K. — length 21'6"

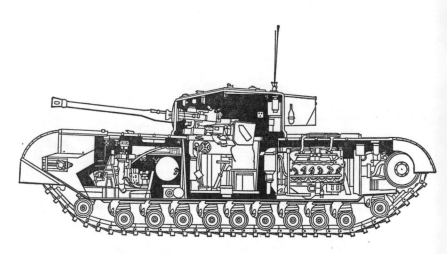

Tank, Infantry, Mark IV, Churchill III, U.K. — length 24'5"

different chassis and weapons must have created. British S.P. weapons were fewer and more standardized, the Canadian 25-pr Sexton being one of the best. American policy, after early efforts on wheeled and half-tracked chassis, was generally to standardize on tank chassis. Some American S.P.s— notably the 105-mm. (Priest) and 3-in. M.10 were also used by British forces. Powerful and well-armoured Soviet S.P. guns were mounted on T-34, KV and JS chassis.

Wheeled armoured vehicles, as in earlier stages of the war, continued to be developed in the greatest variety by the British Commonwealth countries. A version of the useful Daimler Scout Car was built in Canada (and even in prototype form in Italy, where British A.F.V.s were admired) together with light and medium armoured cars. India and South Africa also built in quantity wheeled armoured vehicles using Canadian automotive parts.

The British Daimler armoured car was probably the best Allied armoured car of World War II, being compact and manœuvrable and with a reasonably good cross-country performance as well as being better armoured and armed than most German armoured cars. The German eight-wheelers were powerful and of excellent mechanical design but clumsy by British standards.

The half-track continued to the end of the war to be a characteristic German vehicle, the armoured 1-ton and 3-ton variants still being used in large numbers, although basically infantry-carrying or support vehicles. Many comparable functions were carried out in British units by small full-tracked armoured vehicles of the Universal Carrier type. Half-tracks were also produced in small numbers by Japan and in large quantities for the Allies by the United States. The U.S. half-tracks, almost all of which were armoured. were relatively straight-forward designs but had one advantage over their German opposite numbers in having a driven front axle

This wide variety of tracked, wheeled and half-tracked armoured vehicles was produced in staggering quantities by the countries at war, production rising (even in Germany under heavy Allied air attack) to a peak in 1944–45, so that, for example, the United States alone had built by the end of the war nearly 89,000 tanks.

A description of each of the following coloured plates commences on page 93 and ends on page 154.

1
Tankette, Type 97 (Te-Ke) (*above*) and Light Tank, Type
95 (Ha-Go)

Japan

2
Medium Tank, Type 97 (Shinhoto Chi-Ha) (*above*) and
Medium Tank, Type 3 (Chi-Nu)

3
Medium Tank, Type 4 (Chi-To) (*above*) and Medium
Tank, Type 5 (Chi-Ri)

4
Gun Tank, Type 1 (Ho-Ni I) (*above*) and 15-cm. S.P.
Howitzer, Type 4 (Ho-Ro)

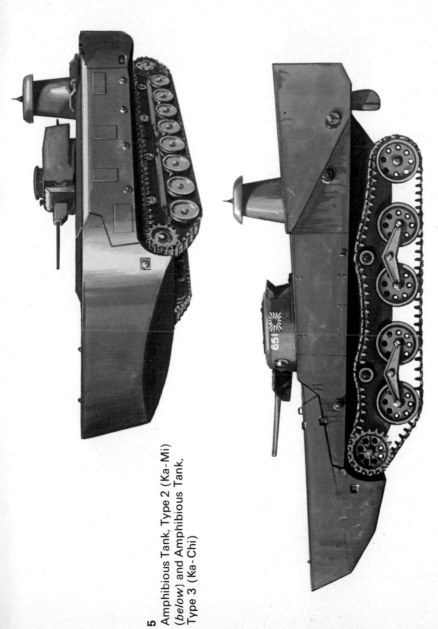

5 Amphibious Tank, Type 2 (Ka-Mi) (*below*) and Amphibious Tank, Type 3 (Ka-Chi)

6
Flail Tank (*above*), and Engineer Vehicle—Jungle Cutter
(Ho-K)

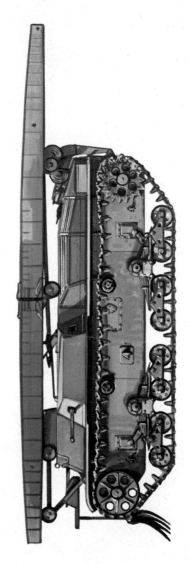

7
Tank Recovery Vehicle, Type E (*below*) and Tank Bridge-layer (Medium Type 97 chassis)

8
Armoured Personnel Carrier, Half-tracked, Type 1 (Ho-Ha)
(*below*) and Armoured Personnel Carrier, Tracked, Type 1
(Ho-Ki)

9
Light Tank M.5A1 (*below*) and 75-mm. Howitzer Motor
Carriage, M.8

10
Light Tank, M.22 (Locust) (*below*) and Light Tank, M.24
(Chaffee)

11
Medium Tank, M.3 (Lee) (*above*) and Tank, Medium,
Grant

12
Medium Tank, M.4 (typical) (*below*) and Sherman Vc

13
Medium Tank, M.26 (Pershing)

14
Heavy Tanks, M.6 (*above*) and M.6A1

15
105-mm. Howitzer Motor Carriage, M.7 (*above*), and as
'S.P. 105-mm. Priest' (*below*)

U.S.A.

16
3-in. Gun Motor Carriage, M.10 (*above*) and 76-mm. Gun
Motor Carriage, M.18

17
Landing Vehicle, Tracked (Unarmored) Mark IV (LVT4)
(*below*) and Landing Vehicle, Tracked (Armored), Mark
IV (LVT[A]4)

U.S.A.

18
Car, Half-Track M.2A1 (*below*) and 75-mm. Gun Motor
Carriage, M.3

19
Armored Car, Staghound I
(T.17E1) (*below*) and
Armored Car, Boarhound (T.18E2)

20
Light Armored Car, M.8 (*above*)
and Armored Utility Car, M.20

21
Tank, Light, Mark VII, Tetrarch (*below*)
and Tank, Light, Mark VIII, Harry Hopkins

22
Tanks, Cruiser, Mark VI, Crusader I (*above*) and Crusader III

23
Tanks, Cruiser, Centaur IV (*below*) and Cromwell

U.K.

24
Tank, Cruiser, Challenger

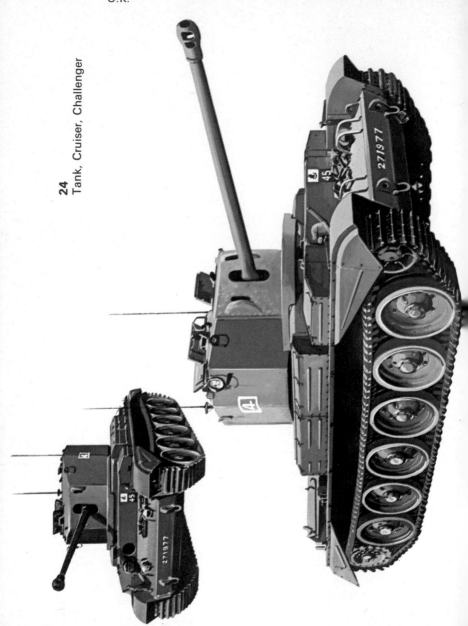

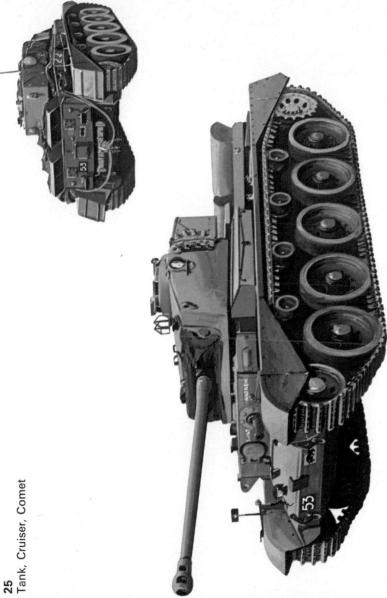

25
Tank, Cruiser, Comet

26
Tank, Cruiser, Ram II (*above*) and Armoured Personnel
Carrier, Ram Kangaroo

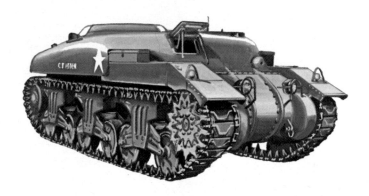

27
Australian Cruiser Tanks, Mark I (*above*) and Mark III

U.K.

28
Tanks, Infantry, Mark IV, Churchill III *(below)* and Churchill VII

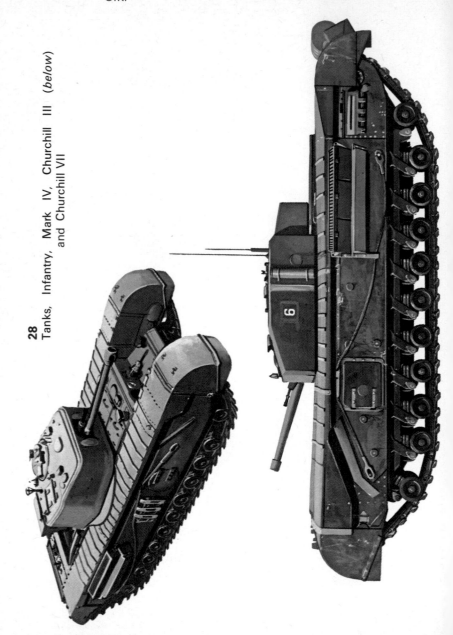

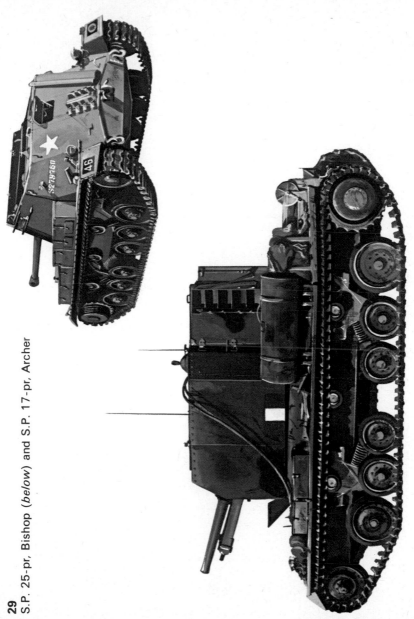

S.P. 25-pr, Bishop (*below*) and S.P. 17-pr, Archer

Canada

30
S.P. 25-pr, Sexton

U.K.

31
Sherman D.D.

32
Churchill VII Crocodile (*below*) and Grant C.D.L.

33
Matilda Scorpion Mark I (*below*) and Grant Scorpion
Mark IV

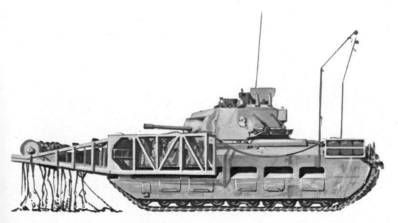

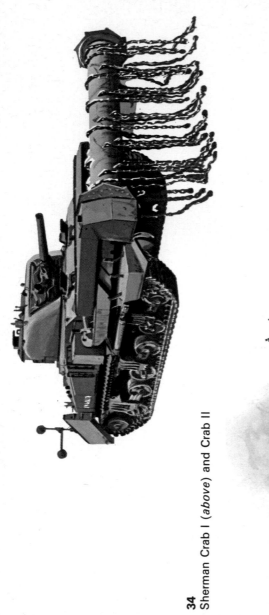

34

Sherman Crab I (*above*) and Crab II

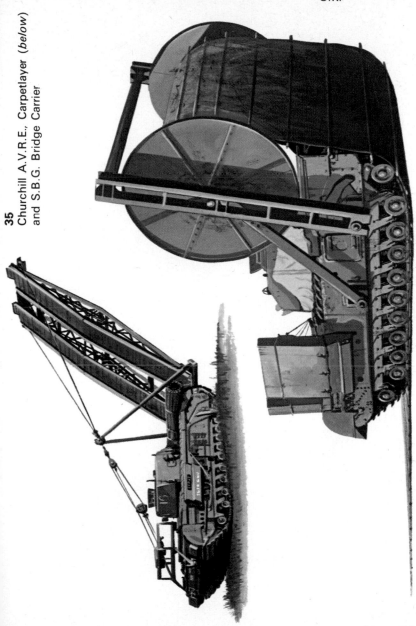

U.K.

35
Churchill A.V.R.E., Carpetlayer (*below*)
and S.B.G. Bridge Carrier

36
Churchill A.R.V., Mark I (*below*) and Sherman B.A.R.V.

37
Carrier, Universal, Mark II (*below*) and Carrier, 2-pr, Tank
Attack (Aust.)

38
South African Armoured Reconnaissance Cars, Mark IV
(*below*) and Mark VI

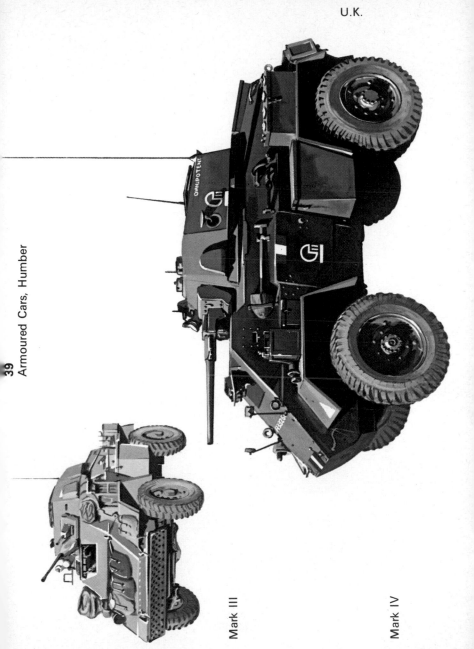

Mark III

Mark IV

U.K.

Mark I

40
Armoured Cars, Daimler

Mark II

41
Armoured Cars, A.E.C.,

U.K.

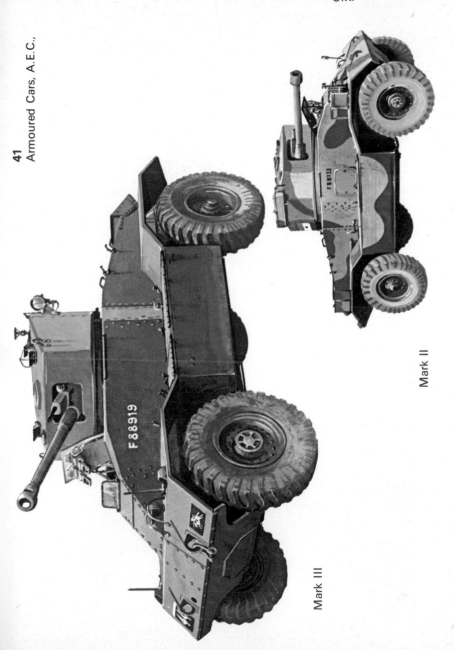

Mark II

Mark III

F 88919

42
Car, Scout, Humber, Mark I

43
Car, Scout, Ford, Lynx II (*above*) and Car, Light Reconnaissance, Canadian G.M., Mark I, Otter I

44

Cars, 4 × 4, Light Reconnaissance, Humber, Mark IIIA (*below*) and Morris, Mark II

45

Armoured Carrier, Wheeled, I.P., A.O.V.

Armoured Carrier, Wheeled, I.P., Mark IIA

U.K.

46 Armoured Command Vehicle (A.E.C.) 4 × 4, Mark I

Armoured Command Vehicle (A.E.C.) 6 × 6, Mark I

47

S.P. 17-pr Gun—Straussler

Carrier, A.E.C., 6-pr Gun, Mark I (Deacon)

48
Ford Armoured Cars (Arab Legion)—'2nd type' (*below*)
and '3rd type'

France

Autocanon Dodge (*below*) and Autocanon 75-mm., Ford

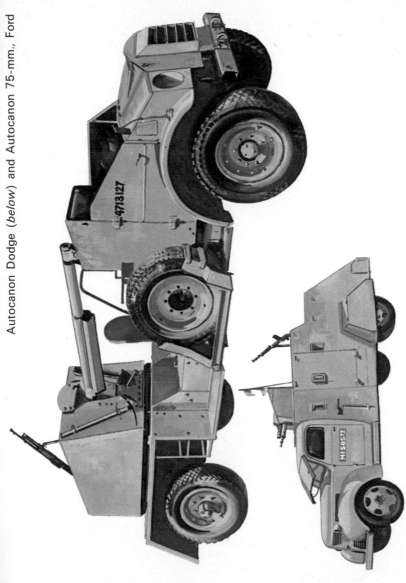

50
Carro Armato M.15/42

51
Carro Armato P.40

Italy

52 Semovente M.42M da 75/34 (*above*) and Semovente
M.42L da 105/23

53
Panzerkampfwagen II, Ausf. L, Luchs

Germany

54
Panzerkampfwɛgen III, Ausf. L (*below*) and Ausf. M

55
Panzerkampfwagen IV, Ausf. H

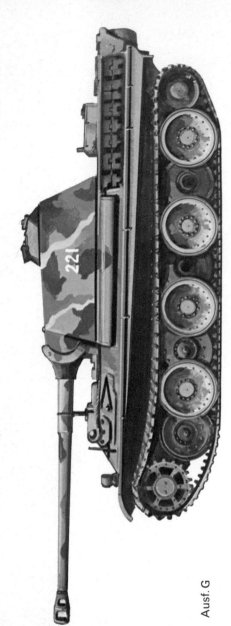

Ausf. G

56
Panzerkampfwagen V, Panther, Ausf. D

57
Panzerkampfwagen VI, Tiger I

58 Panzerkampfwagen VI, Tiger II with Porsche turret (*below*) and standard turret

Germany

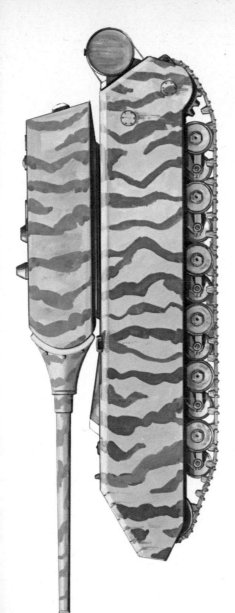

59
Panzerkampfwagen Maus

Panzerkampfwagen E.100

Jagdpanzer 38(t), Hetzer

61
Sturmgeschütz III/10.5-cm. StuH

Germany

62
Sturmpanzer IV, Brummbär (*above*) and Jagdpanzer
IV/70

63
8.8-cm. Panzerjäger Panther-Jagdpanther

64
Jagdpanzer Tiger (P), Elefant

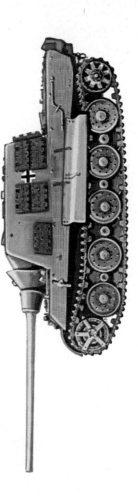

65 Jagdpanzer VI Jagdtiger with Porsche suspension (*above*) and Henschel suspension

66
7.5-cm. Pak auf Gw. 38(t), Marder III, Ausf. M

67
15-cm. sIG33 auf Sf. II (*above*) and 7.62-cm. Pak auf
Gw. II, Ausf. D

68
15-cm. Pz fH 18 auf Gw. III/IV, Hummel (*below*) and
8.8-cm. Pak 43/1 (L/71) auf Gw. III/IV, Nashorn

69
Flakpanzer IV (3.7-cm.), Möbelwagen (*below*) and
Flakpanzer IV (2-cm.), Wirbelwind

70
Schwerer Ladungsträger (Sdkfz 301) (*above*)
and Leichter Ladungsträger (SdKfz 302)

71
Leichter Schützenpanzerwagen SdKfz 250/8 (*below*) and
Leichter Schützenpanzerwagen SdKfz 250/9

72
Panzerspähwagen SdKfz 234/2 (Puma) (*above*) and
Panzerspähwagen SdKfz 234/3

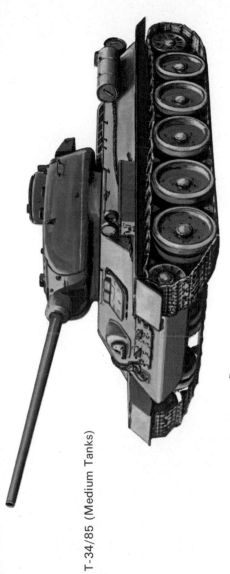

T-34/85 (Medium Tanks)

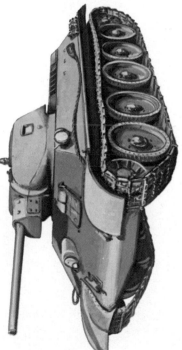

73
T-34 ('T-34/76B')

74
KV-85 (Heavy Tank) (*above*) and SU-85

75
JS-II (Heavy Tank)

76
JSU-122 (*above*) and JSU-152

U.S.S.R.

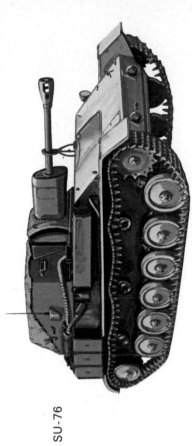

SU-76

77
KT (Winged Tank)

78
BA-64 (Light Armoured Car)

79
Tanque 'Narhuel', Modelo DL 43

80
Stridsvagn M/42 (*below*) and Stormartillerivagn M/43

TANKS AND OTHER
ARMOURED FIGHTING VEHICLES

1 Tankette, Type 97 (Te-Ke) and Light Tank, Type 95 (Ha-Go), Japan.

The ultra-light tank was evolved in Japan for a dual purpose—as an infantry supply vehicle (towing a trailer) and as a command and liaison vehicle for tank units. Derived originally from Carden-Loyd designs (examples of which were purchased from Britain) and developed through the Type 95 Tankette series, more emphasis was placed on the second function with the Type 97, as the Tankette was found to be quite a useful fighting vehicle, except against heavier enemy tanks. A two-man 4·25-ton vehicle, built by Tokyo Motor Industry, the Type 97 had a 60-b.h.p. Ikegai air-cooled diesel engine at the rear to the right, a centrally mounted turret with a 37-mm. gun and the driver was located at the front left-hand side. The track-driving sprockets were at the front and the suspension consisted, each side, of a large trailing idler wheel and two two-wheel bogie units on bell-crank arms restrained by a long horizontal coil spring.

The light tank was produced to meet a demand for a lighter and more mobile tank than the Type 89 Medium for use in mechanized formations. Designed by Mitsubishi Heavy Industries Ltd in 1933, the Type 95 was the first Japanese light tank classified as such and, due to delays in the introduction of later models into production, remained the principal light tank in service throughout World War II.

The official name for this tank was Ha-Go, but it was often known colloquially as 'Kyo-Go' ('ninety-five'). One of its principal features was the air-cooled diesel engine, able to function satisfactorily in the extreme cold of north Manchuria or in tropical climates. This six-cylinder unit of 110-b.h.p. was located at the rear at the right. Another feature was the use of welding in the construction of the armoured hull, which was protected on a 12-mm. basis. The armament of the Type 95 Light Tank consisted of a 37-mm. gun in the turret (manned by the commander) with, additionally, a ball-mounted 7·7-mm. machine-gun at the right side near the back and another 7·7-mm. machine-gun in a ball mounting at the front left-hand side of the hull. The third member of the crew, the driver, sat to the right of the hull machine-gunner. The transmission layout and bell-crank suspension of the Type 95 were similar to those of the Type 97 Tankette. An interesting point with the Type 95 is that tanks used in north Manchuria were modified while they were there so that the bell crank suspension arms were inverted and an extra small road wheel introduced at the centre of each arm. This was to counteract pitching encountered in the furrows of the kaolin fields of the country.

Both the Type 97 Tankette and the Type 95 Light Tank were used widely in World War II. The former was quite effective when used in comparable functions to those of the British Universal Carrier series. The latter, although obviously no match for Allied medium tanks, was a good vehicle in its class and one of the best Japanese tanks of its era.

2 Medium Tank, Type 97 (improved) (Shinhoto Chi-Ha) and Medium Tank, Type 3 (Chi-Nu), Japan.

The first tank built in Japan was a prototype completed in 1927 which was developed into a heavy tank. A second and lighter prototype was classified as a medium, which was standardized as Type 89. The design of the latter was directly influenced to some extent by a Vickers Mark C medium tank purchased from Britain. An indirect effect was a fire in the petrol engine of the British tank, which led to the important decision by the Japanese to develop a tank diesel engine, for economy as well as its low fire risk. Air cooling of the diesel was decided on for its advantages in cold climates and in avoiding problems of water supply.

The Type 89 gave good service but by 1935 developments in other countries made it desirable to introduce a faster medium tank, better-protected without undue increase in weight.

The more successful of two competing designs was adopted in 1937 as the Type 97 medium tank or Chi-Ha. With a new suspension system of medium-sized road wheels carried on internal bell cranks controlled by horizontal coil springs, and a cleaned-up hull design, the Type 97 foreshadowed the general appearance of most modern tanks. The main armament still consisted of the short-barrelled 57-mm. gun, however, and an improved model of Type 97 was designed in which the original turret was replaced by a new turret mounting a 47-mm. gun with a much higher velocity than the old 57-mm. gun. Type 97s were reworked with the new turret and the Type 97 modified and known as Shinhoto ('new turret') Chi-Ha became from 1942 onwards the most important Japanese medium tank of World War II. The secondary armament consisted of a machine-gun in the rear face of the turret at the left-hand side and another in the hull front, to the left of the driver.

With a 170-b.h.p. twelve-cylinder diesel engine and weighing just under 16 tons, the Type 97 (improved) had a maximum speed of 23 m.p.h.

Prior to the modifications to Type 97 described above, an improved medium tank, known as Type 1 (Chi-He) was designed. This differed little in layout and external appearance from the Type 97 (improved) except that it had a flat driver's plate, without the curved protruberance of the earlier tank. The Type 1, however, had the maximum armour protection increased from the inadequate 25-mm. of the Type 97 to 50-mm. and the engine was the new standardized air-cooled diesel of 240-b.h.p. giving an increase in speed to 25 m.p.h.

All the features of the Type 1 were included in the Type 3 medium tank of 1943, in which a more powerful gun (by then essential) was also incorporated. This new gun requiring a larger turret, made possible fortunately without major changes because of forethought in the design of the Type 97, which allowed for a larger turret ring than was immediately necessary, was a 75 mm. weapon. Early medium tanks

Type 3 had a gun based on the Type 95 field gun; later tanks a gun developed from the Type 90 field gun. The latter had a higher muzzle velocity with a consequently shorter barrel life. Welded construction introduced in the Type 97 was used largely in the Type 3 medium.

Lack of industrial capacity in Japan in 1943–45 meant that relatively few of the later types of medium tanks could be produced and so the 'new turret' Type 97 remained the chief type in use to the end of the war.

3 Medium Tank, Type 4 (Chi-To) and Medium Tank, Type 5 (Chi-Ri), Japan.

To meet the requirement for a medium tank with a more powerful gun and greater protection, the Type 4 was developed. Armour thickness was increased to a maximum of 75-mm. and the powerful Type 88 75-mm. anti-aircraft gun was adapted for tank use. These features meant increased weight up to about 30 tons, so that the chassis of the Type 97 could no longer be used and a lengthened chassis with the same type of suspension but with seven road wheels each side was designed. To ensure that performance was maintained, the 400-b.h.p. supercharged twelve-cylinder V-form air-cooled diesel engine was used. The top speed of 28 m.p.h. was, in fact, better than that of the Type 3.

Development began in 1944 of what proved to be the ultimate Japanese medium tank of World War II. This, the Medium Type 5, was an outgrowth of the Type 4 but as it was even heavier, weighing 37 tons, an extra road wheel each side was added to the suspension, which still employed the system employed in the Type 97 medium.

The turret of the Type 5 medium had the same 75-mm. main armament as that of the Type 4 but the Type 5 had, in addition, a 37-mm. gun mounted in the front of the hull at the left-hand side. Two machine-guns completed the armament.

In order to get Type 5 mediums into the field as soon as possible, when the invasion of Japan was imminent, a German-designed BMW aircraft air-cooled petrol engine was adapted and used, pending the development of the Japanese diesel engine of the requisite horse power. The BMW engine was of 550-b.h.p. and gave a top speed of 28 m.p.h.

Only the prototype of the Type 5 medium had been completed when World War II ended. A small number of Type 4 mediums had been built and these were not sent overseas but allocated for the defence of Japan.

The illustration of the Medium, Type 5, shows the prototype as it existed without the front track guards and the turret (facing to the rear) minus the 75-mm. gun.

4 Gun Tank, Type 1 (Ho-Ni I) and 15-cm. S.P. Howitzer, Type 4 (Ho-Ro), Japan.

These two self-propelled weapons were both built on the ubiquitous chassis of the Type 97 medium tank, powered with a 170-b.h.p. air-cooled diesel engine. Both were armed with field weapons mounted behind three-sided shields, open at the rear and with only partial overhead protection.

The Ho-Ni I was equipped with a 75-mm. gun Type 90 with a muzzle velocity of 2,260 feet per second and was the only really effective anti-tank weapon available in the field in any quantity. The fixed shield permitted a total traverse of 20 degrees, elevation of 25 degrees and depression of 5 degrees.

A Type 38 15-cm. howitzer equipped the Ho-Ro. This short calibre weapon (12 calibres long) fired a 79-lb high explosive projectile to a maximum range of 6,500 yards. This vehicle formed part of the field artillery element of Japanese armoured formations.

5 Amphibious Tank, Type 2 (Ka-Mi) and Amphibious Tank, Type 3 (Ka-Chi), Japan.

Japan, an island country with widespread interests in the Pacific area in World War II, developed, as might be expected, a number of types of amphibious tanks and support vehicles. One of the most widely used amphibious tanks was the Ka-Mi, which was based on the Light Tank Type 95. The general layout of the Type 95 was retained and the suspension system was identical except that in the amphibious tank the idler was in contact with the ground. The hull, however, was made more box-like, with straight sides, thus increasing the volumetric capacity and hence, inherent buoyancy although the main amphibious capability was provided by two pontoons, one at the front and one at the rear. Propulsion in water was by means of two propellers driven by a power take-off from the engine, a six-cylinder 110-h.p. diesel. Steering in water was by means

of twin rudders attached to the rear pontoon. The freeboard in smooth water was only about 6 inches or so and a tall trunk was fitted over the engine grill as well, occasionally, as a cylindrical extension to the turret cupola. The pontoons could quickly be jettisoned once the tank came ashore.

The armament of the Ka-Mi was one 37-mm. gun and a coaxial machine-gun and the armour was to a maximum of 12-mm. A large crew (for a light tank) of five men was carried, including a mechanic to oversee the land and water power and transmission system. The tank had a speed of 23 m.p.h. on land and 6 m.p.h. on smooth water.

The Amphibious Tank, Type 3, Ka-Chi was a medium equivalent of the Ka-Mi and shared many of its characteristics. From the point of view of the armament it was equivalent to the Medium Type 97 (improved) with its 47-mm. gun and two machine-guns, although mechanically, with a lengthened suspension system with eight road wheels each side and a 240-h.p. Type 100 diesel engine, it had more in common with some of the later Japanese medium tanks. Weighing nearly 29 tons, the Ka-Chi had a water speed of 6 m.p.h. and a road speed of 20 m.p.h. Unlike the light amphibious tank, it is not known to have been employed in action.

The illustrations show both types complete with fore and aft pontoons and with engine air trunks fitted.

6 Flail Tank and Engineer Vehicle —Jungle Cutter (Ho-K), Japan.

These two interesting examples of Japanese specialized armour were both based on the widely used Type 97 medium tank.

The flail tank was intended to clear anti-tank mines by detonation through the beating action of the flail attached to the revolving drum. The type of drive used for the flails is not known, except that it was presumably by means of a power take-off from the tank's own engine, since an auxiliary engine was apparently not carried. The tank was normal in most other respects and retained its turret. This vehicle is not known to have been used in action and may not have progressed beyond the prototype stage.

The jungle cutter was a device developed only by the Japanese. It consisted of a wedge-shaped pointed attachment, rather like the bow of a speed boat in appearance, which was carried at the front of the turretless engineer vehicle. Slightly wider than the vehicle to which it was attached, the device was used for forcing a way through heavy undergrowth. The point of attachment of the jungle cutter was at two lugs on the glacis plate of the engineer vehicle. It could be raised from the normal horizontal position if necessary and is shown raised in the illustration.

An alternative attachment for the engineer vehicle was a conventional bulldozer blade.

7 Tank Recovery Vehicle, Type E and Tank Bridgelayer (Medium Type 97 chassis), Japan.

The Japanese developed several types of engineer tanks in World War II, some of which were equipped to carry out apparently on the same mission, a bewildering variety of tasks.

One of the earlier of these vehicles was the Type E, intended for tank recovery but, as adjuncts to this function, equipped as a bridgelayer, flamethrower and mine-clearer. The bridge, about 23 feet long and capable of being folded in two, was normally carried opened above the hull of the vehicle on rollers, by means of which it was launched and then finally pushed into position. Some vehicles of this type were equipped with two hinged forks, with four tines each, one fork in front of each track. These were for mine clearance and also possibly for use as earth anchors. The Type E vehicle also had provision for five flamethrowers, with one mounting at the front and two each side. There was also a machine-gun in a ball mounting in the top centre of the glacis plate. No turret was fitted: armour was to a maximum of 25-mm. It must be assumed that the Type E was intended for special tank recovery tasks in which its particular array of equipment was needed. No jib, or even a winch, seems to have been carried and it seems likely that on some occasions vehicles of this type would have been used in conjunction with other types of engineer vehicles having the necessary pulling or lifting ability.

The suspension of the Tank Recovery vehicle was, surprisingly, quite different from that of any Japanese tank and consisted of eight small road wheels each side, carried in two sets of four (each of two two-wheel bogie units), each set mounted on a semi-elliptic leaf spring. The vehicle was powered by a six-cylinder diesel engine of 140-h.p., giving a maximum speed of 18 m.p.h.

The standard Type 97 medium tank chassis was used for the second engineer vehicle shown here, which was a specialist bridgelayer. The bridge, about 30 feet long, was carried above the hull (the vehicle was turretless) on rollers. It was launched by means of rockets attached to the front end of each trackway.

The illustrations show (top) a bridgelayer facing right and a tank recovery vehicle, Type E, complete with bridge, facing left.

8 Armoured Personnel Carrier, Half-tracked, Type 1 (Ho-Ha) and Armoured Personnel Carrier, Tracked, Type 1 (Ho-Ki), Japan.

Several types of armoured personnel carriers were developed by Japan in World War II, both full-tracked and half-tracked. One of each variety is shown here and they have an affinity in that virtually the same track assembly was used in both.

The half-tracked vehicle Ho-Ha was on the general lines of the German SdKfz 251 series but somewhat larger and of far less sophisticated design. It weighed about 7 tons, was protected by armour up to 8-mm. only and could carry fifteen men. It was powered by a six-cylinder 134-h.p. diesel engine. The suspension consisted of four road wheels each side, with the drive sprockets at the front and the idler wheel at the rear.

The full-tracked armoured personnel carrier Ho-Ki used the same track assembly as the half-track vehicle

except that it had two return rollers instead of one and a rear drive sprocket, the transmission being led back from the six-cylinder 134-h.p. diesel engine mounted at the front. Weighing 6½ tons, the tracked personnel carrier could also carry fifteen men, who were protected by 6-mm. armour all round, although the rear compartment had no overhead protection. A similar vehicle was used as a field artillery tractor.

9 Light Tank, M.5A1 and 75-mm. Howitzer Motor Carriage, M.8, U.S.A.

The Cadillac Division of the General Motors Corporation entered into tank production early in 1942 with a new version of the M.3 Light Tank, known as the M.5. This tank, at the suggestion of Cadillac's, was powered by two eight-cylinder V-form Cadillac automobile engines, with Cadillac Hydramatic automatic transmission. A prototype was constructed in October 1941 by conversion of a standard M.3 and after a highly successful five-hundred mile demonstration drive, the design, subject to modifications in detail, was accepted. A total of 2,074 was built by the end of 1942, when the M.5 was succeeded by an improved model M.5A1. This tank was distinguished from the M.5 chiefly by a turret with an extension at the rear for radio. Other improvements included an escape hatch in the floor of the hull, a gun mount including a direct sight telescope, extra turret periscopes and an anti-aircraft machine-gun mount on the right-hand side of the turret protected by a curved armoured shield. The latter, however, was invariably removed on M.5A1s supplied to the British Army (by whom they were known as Stuart VIs) and sometimes, also, on U.S. Army vehicles. Production of the M.5A1 was ended in mid-1944 when 6,810 had been built.

The M.5A1 (and the M.5) was similar in most respects to the earlier M.3. It had a similar overall performance, in spite of being some 2 tons heavier, with thicker armour, but was much easier to drive than the M.3. The armament consisted of a 37-mm. gun with a coaxial 0·30-in. Browning machine-gun and another in the hull front, together with the anti-aircraft machine-gun already mentioned. An M.5A1 of the U.S. Marine Corps in the Pacific theatre of war is shown in the illustration.

A variant of the M.5 light tank was the Howitzer Motor Carriage M.8. This used the same chassis with the upper hull modified to take an open-topped turret with full traverse, mounting a 75-mm. howitzer. Few changes were found to be necessary beyond removing the ball-mounted hull machine-gun and transferring the driver's and co-driver's hatches to the glacis plate, where they would not interfere with the traverse of the turret.

Known as General Scott, 1,778 M.8s were built between 1942 and 1944 and issued mainly as close support vehicles in Headquarters companies of U.S. armoured battalions in Europe. They were also used by Fighting French troops and one belonging to the French in the Italian campaign, is shown in the illustration.

10 **Light Tank, M.22 (Locust) and Light Tank, M.24 (Chaffee), U.S.A.**

The M.22 was specially designed by the Marmon Herrington Company Inc. as an airborne light tank. The first pilot model was given the experimental designation T.9, and this was followed by two more modified pilot vehicles (T.9E1) late in 1942. After a number of design changes production began in April 1943 and a total of 830 was built by February 1944, by which time the tank was classified 'limited standard' as M.22.

With a layout conventional for medium tanks of the period, the M.22 had a 162-b.h.p. Lycoming engine at the rear, with a 4-speed gearbox and drive to front track sprockets. The driver sat at the front left-hand side. The turret, carrying the other two crew members, was centrally mounted and had a 37-mm. gun coaxial with a 0·30-in. Browning machine-gun. Armour protection was at a maximum of 1 in. and the top speed was 40 m.p.h.

No M.22's were used by the U.S. Army in action and by December 1944 it was decided that there was no need for an airborne light tank. Some M.22's had, however, been supplied to the United Kingdom (where they were named Locusts) and a very small number was used by the British 6th Airborne Division at the Rhine crossing operation in March 1945. Like its British counterpart, the Tetrarch light tank, the Locust's gun was fitted with a Littlejohn Adaptor, converting it to a 'squeeze gun' and greatly increasing the velocity of the projectile. It is not known if Locusts so equipped were used in action, although Tetrarchs with

Littlejohn Adaptors certainly were. A British Locust with the Littlejohn Adaptor is shown in the illustration.

The Light Tank M.24 was the replacement for the M.3–M.5 series which, by 1943, were already considered inadequate, not only in fire power but in other qualities, such as lack of crew space and poor cooling. The layout of the new tank was worked out by the Cadillac Division of the General Motors Corporation in 1943 and Cadillac later became the main producers, together with Massey-Harris —4,070 being built between April 1944 and June 1945.

The most important feature of the M.24, compared with its light tank predecessors, was the adoption of a 75-mm. gun. This was a light weight high velocity (2,050 feet per second) weapon, adapted from aircraft use. It shared a mounting in the turret with a 0·30-in. Browning machine-gun. The twin V-8 Cadillac engine power unit of 220 b.h.p. used successfully in the M.5A1, was adapted for the M.24 and the torsion bar suspension system (with five medium-sized road wheels) was that used on the M.18 gun motor carriage. A crew of five was carried, of which the driver sat at the front left-hand side, with the co-driver-cum-radio operator at the right, where he controlled a ball-mounted 0·30-in. Browning machine-gun in the glacis plate. Separate emergency driving controls were provided for the co-driver. The commander, gunner and loader occupied the turret.

Although only lightly armoured (maximum 1 inch), the Chaffee was a fast, efficient reconnaissance vehicle. During World War II they saw service only at the end of the North West European and Pacific campaigns in 1945, although they were supplied to many different countries in the post-war years. An M.24 of the U.S. Army as it appeared in snow camouflage in North West Europe in the winter of 1944–45 is illustrated.

11 Medium Tank, M.3 (Lee and Grant), U.S.A.

By 1940, the United States had developed a medium tank that was mechanically satisfactory and carried a liberal supply of machine-guns for infantry support. After study of the reports of the German campaign of that year, however, it was felt that the tank's main armament of a 37-mm. gun was inadequate and it was decided to introduce the 75-mm. gun. The existing medium tank M2A1 was taken as the basis and the design modified to carry a 75-mm. gun in the right-hand side of the hull but retaining a turret mounting a 37-mm. gun.

This tank, which in its production form became known as Medium, M.3, had the disadvantage that the 75-mm. gun in the hull had only a limited traverse, but it was accepted that this was only an interim design that would be put into production as quickly as possible in order to get appreciable numbers of new medium tanks into the hands of the troops. For the first time, the enormous resources of the American automotive industry were to be used for tank production and an initial order for 1,000 M.3s to be built at a new tank arsenal at Detroit was awarded even before the factory was built. However, the first M.3 proto-type from the Detroit Tank Arsenal was completed in April 1941, only a short time after prototypes from the more traditional heavy industry tank suppliers, the American Locomotive Co. and Baldwin Locomotive works. Nearly 5,000 M.3s of the original type were built by these and other manu-facturers, the last being delivered in August 1942.

In the meantime, a British purchasing mission in the United States had ordered M.3 mediums in quantity, as well as light tanks. The tanks made to British orders, and subsequently named Grants, had some special modifications, the principal of which were incorpo-rated in the turret. This did not have the cupola, incorporating a machine-gun, on top and there was an overhang at the rear to incorporate the wireless equipment, in accordance with British practice. Lack of a command cupola and turret overhang were both con-sidered to be deficiencies in design later in the war but the lowering of the M.3's considerable height was, no doubt, on balance an advantage, particularly in the open North African terrain where most of the tanks were to go.

The M.3 in its original (and, numeri-cally, by far the most important) ver-sion was powered by a Continental nine-cylinder radial air-cooled engine of 340-b.h.p. and the hull was of all-riveted construction to a maximum armour thickness of 50-mm. The engine was at the rear, the transmission being led forward to a gear-box along-side the driver and the track drive was via front sprockets. The hull-mounted 75-mm. gun at the right had a total

traverse of 30 degrees and 46 rounds were carried. The turret had a full 360 degree traverse and besides the 37-mm. gun (for which 178 rounds were carried) it had a 0·30-in. Browning machine-gun, coaxially mounted. Standard M.3s also had a further Browning in the cupola on the main turret and two more in the glacis plate at the left, operated by the driver. These hull machine-guns were normally removed in all British-used vehicles and, of course, the Grant did not have the machine-gun cupola, although an anti-aircraft machine-gun was sometimes mounted on the turret roof.

The M.3s suspension used the hori-zontal volute system, already well tried in earlier medium and light tanks. It consisted of three twin-wheel bogie units each side.

The Medium M.3 first saw action (as the Grant) with the British forces in the Western Desert in the spring of 1942. In spite of its design shortcomings, its effective 75-mm. gun mounted in a reliable vehicle with a good degree of mobility (maximum speed 26 m.p.h.) helped considerably to redress the balance against the German armour. A Grant of the 3rd Royal Tank Regiment, one of the first units to receive them, is shown in one of the illustrations.

The U.S. Army also used the M.3 in action in North Africa—in Tunisia. This was in the standard form in which a quantity was also supplied to Britain (where they were known as the Lee) and by which name were, likewise, used in North Africa. M.3s were also employed by British Commonwealth forces in the Burma campaign of 1944; often in hybrid form, where they were commonly referred to as 'Lee/Grants', and were used also by the Australians for home defence. The other illustration shows a later production M.3 (with the longer 40 calibre 75-mm. gun) on issue to the U.S. Army training in Britain in 1942.

12 Medium Tank, M.4 (Sherman), U.S.A.

The Sherman is arguably one of the greatest tanks of World War II, even on numbers alone, because over 58,000 were built. The Sherman was a good straightforward design which proved adaptable, so that armament and armour modification could be introduced to enable it to keep level with its opponents to the end of the war.

Design work on the M.4 as the definitive 75-mm. gun-armed medium tank to replace the medium M.3 model was commenced in March 1941. Many of the elements of the M.3, such as the power unit, transmission and suspension were quite satisfactory and were adopted, but the main feature of the M.4 was the incorporation of the 75-mm. gun in a fully rotating turret. The prototype, known as T.6, was ready by September 1941 and after trials and minor design changes was approved for production commencing in early 1942.

Production of the M.4 in the numbers envisaged would have overrun the supply of Continental engines (as used in the M.3 and original M.4 designs) and so the use of alternative engines, already used in later models of the M.3, and others, was provided for. The most important of these were the General Motors 6046 twelve-cylinder diesel

(two six-cylinder truck engines geared together) used in the M.4A2, the Ford GAA V-8 petrol engine, used in the M.4A3 and the Chrysler A.57 thirty-cylinder petrol engine used in the M.4A4. The latter engine consisted of no less than five six-cylinder truck engines all driving a common crank shaft.

The basic hull shape of all Shermans included a well-sloped glacis plate but the form of construction varied, that of the M.4A1 with a cast, rounded hull being closest to the original design. The M.4 (first in designation sequence but actually the third type to enter production) had an all-welded hull with sharp edges, as did the M.4A2, M4A3 and M.4A4. Some late M.4s, however, had a cast front portion married to the welded rear part of the hull.

Armament of the Sherman consisted originally of a 75-mm. M.3 gun (although short M.2 guns with counterweights were provisionally fitted on some of the very first tanks built) with a coaxial 0·30-in. Browning machine-gun. In the front of the hull was a Browning machine-gun in a ball mounting and, beside it, two more Brownings, fixed to fire forwards only. The latter were eliminated after the early production vehicles. Most tanks in American use had a 0·50-in. Browning machine-gun mounted on a pintle on the turret for anti-aircraft use, although this weapon was not accurate and was commonly discarded in British-used tanks. Changes in the main armament of Shermans during the course of production included the 105-mm. howitzer in place of the 75-mm. gun, and the 76-mm. gun, a long high velocity cannon. These weapons were incorporated in a proportion of tanks during the course of production and some tanks supplied to Britain were modified to take the British 17-pr gun. These were M.4A1s, M.4A3s and M.4A4s but mostly the latter, which were known as the Sherman Vc in Britain. The 105-mm. howitzer tanks were used for close support and the 76-mm. and 17-pr gun versions used to stiffen up the anti-tank fire power of the 75-mm. Shermans.

The Sherman was used by American and British forces on nearly all battle fronts from 1942 onwards and several thousand were supplied to the Russians.

One illustration shows a side view of a typical Sherman armed with the 75-mm. gun and the other a 17-pr-equipped Sherman Vc of a British armoured regiment in Normandy in 1944, where this model was first used in action.

13 Medium Tank, M.26 (Pershing), U.S.A.

Following the abandonment of heavy tanks in the U.S.A., attention was turned to the problem of mounting a 90-mm. gun in a medium tank. A series of experimental tanks was built between 1942 and 1944, trying out various suspension systems, transmissions and other components as well as various guns, including the 90-mm. This series culminated in the T.26E1 completed in January 1944. This tank with some modifications, including a muzzle brake on the 90-mm. gun and increased ammunition stowage, became the T.26E3. By this time the need for a better gun than the 76-mm., the best weapon fitted to M.4 Medium tanks,

was recognized following combat exrience in Normandy. There was, therefore, a demand for a 90-mm. gun tank but the T.26E3, now reclassified as a heavy tank was not yet considered battleworthy as it had been insufficiently tested. Twenty tanks out of the first batch to be built were, however, shipped to Europe for field trials and in January 1945 were now declared battleworthy. Allotted to the 3rd and 9th Armoured Divisions of the U.S. First Army, the tanks were named the General Pershing and standardized as M.26. Production was by now well under way and 200 had been issued by the end of the war in Europe, although most arrived at the front too late to see action. Some that did—at Remagen on the Rhine—were some of the original Pershings issued to the 9th Armoured Division.

The M.26 weighed 46 (U.S.) tons. Besides the 90-mm. gun (53 calibres long) it had a coaxial 0·30-in. Browning machine-gun and another Browning in a ball-mounting in the hull glacis plate and a 0·50-in. anti-aircraft machine-gun on the turret top. The crew of five were protected by armour at a maximum of 102-mm.

The M.26's engine was a Ford Model GAF eight-cylinder V-form type of 500-b.h.p. and the transmission was Torquematic with three forward speeds, with the track drive from rear sprockets. Suspension was of the torsion bar type and a maximum speed of 30 m.p.h. could be attained.

Although arriving too late to see much action in World War II, the Pershing was the direct ancestor of a long line of post-war U.S. medium tanks.

14 Heavy Tank, M.6, U.S.A.

A tank which received much publicity in the Allied press in 1941–42 was the American M.6 heavy tank. Sometimes shown crushing motor cars, the 50-ton M.6 was of spectacular appearance and, for its time, was a powerful tank.

Called for in 1940 as a heavy tank to complement the M.3 Medium, the first pilot model, out of several designed to test alternative forms of hull construction, transmission and power unit, was completed at the end of 1941. This model, T.1E2, had a cast hull and a torque converter transmission and was later standardized as Heavy Tank M.6. The T.1E3, which appeared slightly later, had a welded hull but was otherwise similar, and was standardized as M.6A1. The third to appear, T.1E1, was ready in 1943—this model had electric transmission and a cast hull. It was usually known later as M.6A2.

All models of this heavy tank were powered by a Wright G-200 radial nine-cylinder air-cooled engine of 800-b.h.p. which gave a maximum speed of about 22 m.p.h. The main armament consisted of a 3-in. gun (a modified anti-aircraft gun) with a coaxial 37-mm. gun in the turret. (The T.1E2 had also a 0·30-in. Browning machine-gun in a separate cupola on top and a 0·50-in. machine-gun on a high-angle mounting at the right rear of the turret.) Two 0·50-in. machine-guns were mounted in the front hull plate under the control of the co-driver and the driver was responsible for two (later one) fixed machine-guns. Armour was at a maximum of 100-mm. and a crew of six was carried.

Because of disagreement over the need for a heavy tank, the large orders originally envisaged were reduced drastically to one hundred and fifteen in September 1942 and then cancelled altogether at the end of the year, although there were subsequent experiments with 90-mm. and 105-mm. guns. Consequently, no more than forty of all variants of the M.6 series, including prototypes, were built. Apart from propaganda purposes, however, the programme had involved useful work, which was not wasted, on armour design, gun stabilizers and power traverse, horizontal volute spring suspension and transmissions, as all these features of the M.6 were used in various later light and medium tanks.

The illustrations show the M.6 (T.1E2) and (below) the M.6A1.

15 105-mm. Howitzer Motor Carriage, M.7 (S.P. 105-mm., Priest), U.S.A.

In action for the first time with British forces in North Africa, where it formed an important element in the self-propelled artillery available at the Alamein battle in October 1942, the Howitzer Motor Carriage M.7 became the main field artillery component in U.S. armoured divisions during World War II.

The decision to mount a 105-mm. field howitzer on the same chassis as the M.3 Medium Tank was taken in June 1941. Production began in April 1942, so that the first ninety vehicles for British use were delivered in Egypt in September. A Priest (as they were named by the British) belonging to 11th

Regiment, Royal Horse Artillery (of 1st Armoured Division), which received its first Priests on 10 September 1942, is shown in one of the illustrations. This vehicle has the earlier type of 3-piece noseplate.

The M.7 had the 105-mm. howitzer mounted to the right of the hull centre line to fire forwards, with a total traverse of 45 degrees. The driver sat at the left, and a characteristic dustbin-shaped 'pulpit' mounting for a 0·5-in. Browning machine-gun was at the right. The Continental nine-cylinder radial engine, drive train and suspension were all similar to those of the M.3 medium. Maximum speed was about 25 m.p.h. Armour was at a maximum thickness of 62 mm. although there was no overhead protection for the crew of seven, except for the driver.

A later, but generally similar, version of the M.7, the M.7B1, using M.4 Medium Tank components replaced the former in production from March 1944 onwards until the type was gradually replaced by the M.37 in the last months of the war.

The M.7 was used widely by field artillery units in U.S. armoured divisions from 1942 to 1945 in most theatres of war, including North West Europe. An M.7 in this area as it appeared in late 1944 is shown in one of the coloured views. After the North African campaign Priests continued in American and British use in the Sicilian and Italian campaigns which followed (and during which, incidentally, a 10-in. mortar was experimentally fitted in one). They were also employed by British troops in the Burma campaign and in the opening stages of the Normandy operations.

16 3-in. Gun Motor Carriage, M.10 and 76-mm. Gun Motor Carriage, M.18, U.S.A.

It was American philosophy in 1942 that enemy tanks should be engaged wherever possible by specialized 'tank destroyers', rather than by their own tanks. The characteristics required of a tank destroyer were a powerful gun and a good speed, even if these were attained at the expense of reduced protection for the crew. The Gun Motor Carriage M.10 was an adaptation of the M.4 Medium Tank chassis based on these principles. The powerful 3-in. gun was mounted in an open-top fully rotating turret on a modified M.4 tank hull with engines, transmission and suspension, equivalent to corresponding vehicles in the M.4 series. The maximum armour thickness was only 37 mm., although the side plates of the hull were, unlike those of the M.4, sloped to give better protection. The M.10 had twin General Motors diesel engines like the Medium Tank M.4A2, and the M.10A1 (externally similar to the M.10) had the Ford GAA eight-cylinder petrol engine, like the M.4A3. In either case, the maximum speed was 30 m.p.h. A development of the M.10 series was the M.36, a similar vehicle but equipped with a 90-mm. gun—the only U.S. armoured vehicle in the field with this weapon and the only one able to tackle the German Tiger II before the advent of the M.26 heavy tank.

Some M.10's and M.10A1's were supplied to the United Kingdom, and they were used by British and Commonwealth forces in Italy and North West Europe. A British modification to a proportion of the vehicles received was the substitution of the 17-pr for the 3-in. gun.

The Gun Motor Carriage M.18 continued the idea behind the M.10 but on a more modern chassis which, because of its weight of around 19 tons with a high power/weight ratio, turned out to be the fastest tracked fighting vehicle of World War II. Up to 55 m.p.h. could be achieved.

After undergoing several changes in both armament and suspension, the M.18, later nicknamed Hellcat, in its final form consisted of a 76-mm. gun, 55 calibres long, mounted in a partly open top turret on a new chassis with torsion bar suspension, powered by a Continental nine-cylinder radial engine of 340 b.h.p. (400 b.h.p. engines in some). The driver sat at the left front of the hull and the co-driver at the right, with the three other crew members in the turret. The commander sat at the left side of the turret, where he was able to operate the 0·50-in. Browning machine-gun carried on a ring mounting on the turret top.

Between July and October 1944, 2,507 M.18's were built, and all went to the U.S. Army where they were employed, with great success, mainly in the Italian and North West European theatres of war. The M.18 chassis was also used for the development of other vehicles, including the M.24 light tank.

17 Landing Vehicle, Tracked (Unarmored) Mark IV (L.V.T.4) and Landing Vehicle, Tracked (Armored) Mark IV (L.V.T.[A]4), U.S.A.

The great majority of amphibious cargo carriers used in World War II were built by the United States; neither her Allies nor her enemies, apart from Japan, paying very much attention to this class of vehicle.

The type was derived from an amphibian designed by Donald Roebling, intended for rescue work in hurricanes and the swampy Everglades region of Florida. A militarized version of Roebling's 1940 model was ordered as a Landing Vehicle Tracked for the U.S. Marine Corps and known as L.V.T.1. A greatly improved model, L.V.T.2, appeared in 1943. The next development, which finally became the L.V.T.3, had twin Cadillac engines in the pontoons at either side, so enabling a rear-loading ramp to be incorporated. The L.V.T.2, which had a single seven-cylinder Continental radial engine, was also modified to provide an unobstructed hold with a rear-loading ramp by having the engine moved forward, the result being known as L.V.T.4.

Armoured cargo and support versions of the L.V.T.'s were also developed, the L.V.T.(A)1 and L.V.T.(A)2, both having a similar chassis to the LVT2, the former being enclosed, with an M.3 light tank turret (37-mm. gun and 0·30-in. Browning machine-gun) mounted on the roof, the latter a cargo carrier only. The L.V.T.(A)4 was similar to the L.V.T.(A)1, except that a 75-mm. howitzer turret from the M.8 gun motor carriage was used.

All the L.V.T. series were propelled in water by means of their tracks, which on all except the original L.V.T.1 had W-shaped grousers added. The water speed for all models was between 6 and 7½ m.p.h. The L.V.T.1 had an unsprung suspension system, but all the later L.V.T.s used an interesting rubber torsion suspension. Each road wheel was mounted independently on an arm, the pivot of which was a hollow tube, fitted over a smaller tube attached to the hull. The space between the two tubes was filled with vulcanized rubber which, in resisting the movement of the tube-carrying road wheel, acted like a spring.

The production of L.V.T.s in the United States amounted to 1,225 L.V.T.1s, 3,413 L.V.T.2s and L.V.T.(A)2s, 509 L.V.T.(A)1s, 1,890 L.V.T.(A)4s and 8,438 L.V.T.4s. The L.V.T.3 appeared late in World War II and was first used in action in April 1945—2,962 were built, many of which saw service after the war. There was also an improved version of the L.V.T.(A)4, the L.V.T.(A)5 with powered turret traverse, of which 269 were built too late to see action.

All the L.V.T.s (except as mentioned above) saw extensive service with the U.S. Army and Marine Corps in the Pacific, taking part in the assaults on the Japanese-held islands. L.V.T.s were also supplied to the British Army (where they were classified as 'Amphibians, Tracked' 2 ton (L.V.T.1 and L.V.T.(A)1) or 2½ ton) by whom they were used in the marshy areas of North Italy, and (in company with American-manned L.V.T.s) in the Rhine and other river crossings in North West Europe. Most of the vehicles used by the British were L.V.T.2s and L.V.T.(A)2s—known usually as Buffalo II—and L.V.T.4 (Buffalo IV). One of the latter, carrying a Universal Carrier, is shown in one illustration. The other picture shows a L.V.T.(A)4 as used by U.S. Forces in the Pacific war theatre in late 1944.

18 Car, Half-Track, M.2A1 and 75-mm. Gun Motor Carriage, M3, U.S.A.

Half-tracks were produced extensively by the United States, as well as Germany, in World War II and used for a variety of purposes. The American vehicles were generally somewhat less sophisticated, both mechanically and in the hull design, than their German counterparts, although they did have driven front axles.

Nearly all the U.S. half-tracks of World War II were armoured and the design originated, in essence, through the addition of rear tracks (of the type developed in France by Citröen from designs by Adolphe Kégresse) to a four-wheel-drive Scout Car, M.3A1. The first standardized model was a personnel carrier for ten men known as Car, Half-Track, M.2.

The layout of the M.2 was typical of the great majority of U.S. half tracks built during World War II. The engine was in the conventional normal-control truck position and the transmission was led, via a transfer box, forward to the front wheels and back to the track drive wheels at the front of the track assembly. The track suspension consisted of four road wheels each side, carried on a single bogie unit. The tracks consisted of continuous bands, made up of steel cables covered with metal cross pieces (to avoid slip) and metal track guides. A roller was carried in front of the radiator to help prevent the vehicle 'ditching'. The armoured hull, bolted on to the chassis frame, was made up of flat plates of 6·35-mm. thickness, except for the driver's plate and the upper, hinged, parts of the side doors, which were 12·72-mm.

The engine in the M.2 was the White six-cylinder in-line type of 147 b.h.p. The armament consisted of one 0·30-in. and one 0·50-in. Browning machine-guns. These weapons could be mounted on a continuous rail which ran round the perimeter of the inside of the hull.

The M.2 was followed by a similar vehicle with a slightly longer hull, capable of carrying thirteen men, designated Personnel Carrier, Half-Track, M.3. Other differences included a rear door and the omission of the machine-gun 'skate rail', a pedestal mount being provided instead. Newer versions of both M.2 and M.3, standardized in 1943, were the M.2A1 and M.3A1, both of which had an armoured ring mount at the front left-hand side of the hull for the 0·50-in. machine-gun for use against aerial or ground targets.

To meet the demand for half-tracks, the International Harvester Company joined the production programme, and the International six-cylinder engine of 143 b.h.p. was used in the M.5 and M.9 series which were externally much like the M.2 and M.3 series.

One of the earliest of many self-propelled gun mountings on half-track chassis, and the first to be standardized, was the Gun Motor Carriage M.3. This was basically a M.3 Personnel Carrier with a 75-mm. gun, model M.1897A4 (originally a French design) mounted with a shield in the crew compartment, where it had a traverse of 19 degrees left and 21 degrees to the right. The gun was intended as an anti-tank weapon, and the projectile had a muzzle velocity of 2,000 feet per second.

U.S. half-tracked 75-mm. gun motor carriages were used in action in Tunisia and Italy before being declared obsolete in September 1944. They were also used by the U.S. Marine Corps in the Pacific theatre and one of these is shown in the illustration. Some vehicles of this type supplied to Britain were used in armoured car regiments for fire support purposes.

Half-tracked personnel carriers were used widely by U.S. forces and their allies. An M.2A1 belonging to the Fighting French is illustrated.

19 Armored Car, Staghound I (T.17E1) and Armored Car, Boarhound (T.18E2), U.S.A.

Relatively few armoured cars were produced in the United States during World War II, because the American preference was for tracked vehicles for most combat tasks, including reconnaissance. However, British experience in the North African desert had shown that good use could be made of armoured cars in this kind of terrain and several American armoured car designs were started in 1941–42, prompted by British needs. The first of these were the T.17 and T.17E1 commenced in June 1941. Both rear-engined armoured cars, equipped with a 37-mm. gun turret (somewhat like that of the Grant medium tank) and generally alike in layout and appearance, the T.17 was a six-wheeled vehicle (6 × 6) by Ford and the T.17E1 was four-wheeled and designed by General Motors (Chevrolet Motor Car Division). Some 3,760 T.17s and 3,500 T.17E1s were on order by June 1942, but in reviewing the overall production of armoured cars, the Special Armored Vehicle Board decided to eliminate the T.17 on the grounds that it was too heavy. Only 250 had been made and these were allocated for internal security duties in the U.S.A. The T.17E1 order was also in danger of being cancelled after 250 were built, but production was continued at the specific request of the United Kingdom, and a final total of 2,844 T.17E1s was built by December 1943, all of which were supplied to Britain or Commonwealth countries, where they were known as Staghound I.

The Staghound was without a chassis as such, the automotive components being attached direct to the armoured hull. The power unit consisted of two six-cylinder G.M.C. Model 270 engines, each of 97 b.h.p., mounted at the rear and driving all four wheels through a Hydramatic (automatic) transmission. The turret carried a 37-mm. gun and a 0·30-in. Browning machine-gun, mounted coaxially, and there was another Browning machine-gun in a ball mount in the glacis plate, controlled by the co-driver at the right. The driver, who enjoyed power steering, sat at the left. Hull armour was at a maximum of $\frac{7}{8}$ inches (22 mm.), although the turret was mainly $1\frac{1}{4}$–$1\frac{3}{4}$ inches thick.

Deliveries of Staghounds to the British forces were too late for them to be used in the Desert fighting, where they would have been ideal. Although easy to drive, they were not popular with armoured car regiments for reconnaissance duties in European terrain, where they were regarded as being too large and lacked the manœuvrability of the smaller British Daimler armoured cars. None the less, Staghounds found useful employment as command vehicles at squadron and regimental headquarters, where their roominess and provision for a crew of five were advantages. (A Staghound belonging to the regimental headquarters of a British armoured car regiment is shown in the illustration.)

A Staghound A.A. armoured car (T.17E2) was also built for Britain and 1,000 of them were produced. This had an open top turret, designed by Frazer-Nash in England and built by the Norge Division of Borg-Warner in Detroit, mounting twin 0·50-in. anti-aircraft machine-guns. British modifications of the Staghound I included the Staghound II, in which the 37-mm. gun was replaced by a 3-in. howitzer for close support use, and the Staghound III, in which a British Crusader cruiser tank 75-mm. gun turret was mounted in place of the original turret.

The heavy armoured car T.18E2 had all the characteristics required for open desert warfare to an even greater degree than the Staghound and, like it, unfortunately was ready only when the campaign in North Africa was over. It weighed over 26 (short) tons and was over 20 feet long, but the armament was only a 6-pr gun and two 0·30-in. Browning machine-guns (one in the glacis plate). This was much inferior to that of many tanks better armoured and weighing less, although with two G.M.C. engines totalling 250 b.h.p. the T.18E2, named Boarhound by Britain, was capable of a speed of 50 m.p.h. Only 30 T.18E2s out of the original order for 2,500 were completed by the Yellow Truck and Coach Company division of General Motors. All of these were delivered to Britain where they were stored in ordnance depots, none being used in action.

20 Light Armored Car, M.8 and Armored Utility Car, M.20, U.S.A.

The best American armoured car of World War II was designed in response to a requirement by the Tank Destroyer Force for a 37-mm. Gun Motor Carriage. Intended to replace the 37-mm. Gun Motor Carriage M.6—an anti-tank gun on an unarmoured ¾-ton truck—the T.22, prototype of the M.8, was later re-classified as a light armoured car.

The T.22 was designed by the Ford Motor Co. in competition with other 6 × 4 and 4 × 4 projects by Studebaker and Fargo. Out of these and many other armoured car designs at this time (some of which had even received large production orders) only the T.17E1 and the T.22, which was completed in early 1942, modified as T.22E2 and standardized as M.8, remained to be produced in quantity after a critical survey had been carried out by the Special Armored Vehicle Board.

A six-wheeled, six-wheel-drive vehicle with a rear-mounted engine—the 110-b.h.p. six-cylinder Hercules JXD—the M.8 had a welded hull (armoured to a maximum of ¾ in.) and a circular cast turret with an open top. The armament consisted of a 37-mm. gun and a 0·30-in. Browning machine-gun in the turret with provision for a 0·50-in. heavy machine-gun to be mounted on the turret top. With a four-speed gear-box, the maximum speed of the M.8 was 55 m.p.h. The car had a four-man crew.

The Armoured Utility Car M.20 was a companion vehicle to the M.8, to which it was mechanically identical. Intended as a command vehicle or armoured personnel or cargo carrier, it differed from the M.8 in having no turret and a square, raised centre section of the hull. This was open-topped and was surmounted by a ring-mounting for a 0·50-in. machine-gun. The M.20 could carry up to six men, according to function.

A total of 8,523 M.8s was built in World War II and 3,791 M.20s. They were used in numbers by the U.S. Army—the M.8 was, in fact, the only armoured car to be employed in action by the Americans. The M.8 (but not the M.20) was also supplied to the United Kingdom for use by the British and Commonwealth armies, by whom they were employed in action chiefly in the Italian campaign towards the end of the war. Named Greyhound in British service, the M.8's characteristics were summarized by one armoured car regiment as having a magnificent cross-country performance; being hard to reverse; difficult to protect against mines (the thin hull floor armour—⅛ inch to ¼ inch—was often reinforced by sandbags) and the useful advantage in a reconnaissance vehicle of being able to cross Class 9 bridges.

The illustrations show an M.8 of the U.S. Army in North West Europe (the fifteenth vehicle in C Troop of a reconnaissance unit) with impedimenta as carried in a campaign, and an M.20 in 'parade ground' condition.

21 Tank, Light, Mark VII, Tetrarch and Tank, Light, Mark VIII, Harry Hopkins, U.K.

The Light Tank, Mark VII, was a drastic departure from earlier light tanks (culminating in the Mark VIc) designed by Vickers-Armstrongs Limited. Although owing something to the track-warping steering device of the Vickers Carriers, the Light Mark VII had an entirely new form of steering in that all four road wheels on both sides could be turned into a curve for steering in a wide radius. This warped the tracks in the direction desired, although for sharper turns steering brakes on either track were brought into action.

Developed from a prototype completed at the end of 1937, the Light Mark VII, later known as Tetrarch, although armoured only up to a maximum of 16 mm., had the main armament of a contemporary British cruiser tank—a 2-pr gun with coaxial 7·92-mm. Besa machine-gun. The Littlejohn Adaptor, to greatly increase the muzzle velocity of the 2-pr was fitted to some Tetrarchs and this device is shown on the vehicle (belonging to 6th Airborne Division) illustrated. Although the first Tetrarchs were delivered in 1940, production (by the Metropolitan-Cammell Carriage and Wagon Company Limited—a Vickers-Armstrongs subsidiary) was seriously interrupted by damage caused by an air raid on the factory and the last of the 171 vehicles built was not delivered until 1942. The first use in action of the Tetrarch was during 1942—some with the Russians, who received a small quantity, and some forming a half squadron in the British attack on Madagascar. The remaining stock of Tetrarchs was then reserved for airborne operations.

The Tetrarch created history on the eve of D-Day 1944 by being glider-landed in Normandy. Only about half a dozen tanks were used, and mainly in a defensive role, but their fire power gave useful support to the parachute troops.

Developed from the Tetrarch and weighing a ton heavier, the Light Tank, Mark VIII, named after President Roosevelt's Lend-Lease administrator, had armour protection up to 38 mm. and the design of the hull and turret was ballistically improved. The Harry Hopkins's armament was the same as the Tetrarch's but the maximum speed was reduced from 40 m.p.h. to 30 m.p.h. Following the Tetrarch in the Metropolitan-Cammell production line, 102 Light Mark VIII's were built. They were never used in action and were the last British light tank before the advent of the Alvis Scorpion in the 1960s

22 Tanks, Cruiser, Mark VI, Crusader I and Crusader III, U.K.

The Crusader arose from a proposal by the Nuffield organization for a 'heavy cruiser' development of their earlier model, Cruiser Mark IV. This the War Office accepted: the pilot model was running in July 1939 and full scale production was under way in 1940.

Although the armour protection was increased to a maximum of 40 mm., an extra pair of road wheels added, the main turret redesigned and an auxiliary turret added, the Cruiser Mark VI had many features of the Cruiser Mark IV. These included the same form of Christie suspension, the 340 b.h.p. Nuffield Liberty engine and the same turret armament. Nevertheless, it proved to be far less reliable than its predecessor, particularly when subjected to desert conditions in North Africa. Mechanically, the engine fan drive and the air cleaner were particular sources of weakness, and the cramped auxiliary turret mounting a single 7·92-mm. Besa machine-gun was unsatisfactory. The Crusader's good speed of nearly 30 m.p.h. was an asset in the desert, though, and was a feature liked by its crews and admired by the Germans and Italians—the latter to the point of building an experimental tank of their own modelled on the Crusader.

The demand for heavier armour led to the introduction of the Crusader II, in which the frontal protection was increased to 49 mm. The auxiliary turret was usually omitted in this model, the aperture plated over and the space created used for extra stowage. (Some Crusader I's were also retrospectively modified in this way.)

The 6-pr gun having by then become available, the Crusader III was designed to use it, and the first tanks of this model came off the production lines in May 1942. Basically the same turret was used, with the mantlet redesigned, but the bigger gun meant a reduction in the crew to three (Crusader I had five men, Crusader II without the auxiliary turret had four.)

A total of 5,300 Crusaders was built by a group of firms under the parentage of Nuffield Mechanizations and Aero Limited. This total includes tanks which were later in the war converted to anti-aircraft tanks and 17-pr gun tractors and chiefly employed in action in the North West Europe campaign. The Crusader I's action was in the North African desert in 1941 and the illustration shows one in the markings used at the end of that year. Crusader III's were used by both the Eighth and First Armies in North Africa, and one belonging to a regiment of 6th Armoured Division of First Army in Tunisia in 1942 is shown.

23 Tanks, Cruiser, Centaur and Cromwell, U.K.

As a successor to the Crusader, a new cruiser tank was planned in 1940 to have much heavier armour, a 6-pr gun, and to greatly improve the power/weight ratio by using a de-rated version of the Rolls-Royce Merlin aero engine. The design was completed but as the new engine could not be ready for some time, the Nuffield organization produced an interim model, known as Cruiser Mark VII (and later as Cavalier), which employed the Nuffield Liberty engine, gearbox, transmission and radiators of the Crusader, for which they were also responsible. The Cavalier (of which the prototype appeared early in 1942) was mechanically rather unreliable and only a few hundred were built. It was, however, redesigned by Leyland Motors Limited, retaining the same engine modified and linked to a Merrit-Brown gearbox. The suspension was also improved, although the armour (a basic 76-mm. frontal protection) and the 6-pr gun, coaxial and hull 7·92-mm.

Besa machine-gun armaments were unchanged. This tank was known as Centaur I. The British 75-mm. replaced the 6-pr gun in Centaur III, and Centaur IV was a close support version armed with the 95-mm. howitzer.

Cavaliers and Centaurs were used mainly in secondary roles in the North West Europe campaign, the former only as an artillery observation post vehicle and the latter mainly as O.P., bulldozer and anti-aircraft tanks. Some eighty Centaur IV's of the Royal Marines Armoured Support Group did, however, see action as gun tanks, both in support of the landings, firing from landing craft offshore, and subsequently in continuing to give fire support inland. A Centaur IV of this formation is shown in the illustration.

The Cromwell appeared as the natural development of the Centaur, which had been designed so that the Nuffield Liberty engine could easily be replaced by the new engine, when the Meteor engine was ready for it. The first batch of Meteors (adapted from the Merlin aero engine) were built by Rolls-Royce (although other manufacturers then assumed production) and the Cromwell was produced in series from January 1943 onwards. After some changes, Leyland Motors Limited some months later became production 'parents' for the Cromwell as well as the Centaur—which was, of course, replaced on the assembly lines by the newer tank as soon as possible. Some Centaurs were later re-engined with Meteors and re-designated as Cromwells.

Running through eight basic Marks, the Cromwells I–III had the 6-pr gun, the IV, V and VII had the 75-mm., and the VI and VIII had the 95-mm. howitzer. The early Cromwells were exceedingly fast, with a maximum speed of 40 m.p.h., but this was governed down to 32 m.p.h. on later models to lengthen the life of the Christie suspension. Welded hull construction was first used in British tanks on the Cromwell V w and VII w, and in these tanks the maximum thickness was increased from 76 mm. to 101 mm. British armoured reconnaissance regiments in North West Europe in 1944–45 were equipped with the Cromwell which, additionally, equipped the armoured brigade of 7th Armoured Division in the earlier stages of the campaign. The illustration shows a Cromwell (with 6-pr gun) of 5 Troop, A Squadron, 15th/19th Hussars in 1943, when it formed part of 9th Armoured Division. This regiment, still equipped with Cromwells, became, in 1944, the Armoured Reconnaissance Regiment of 11th Armoured Division in North West Europe.

24 Tank, Cruiser, Challenger, U.K.

The Challenger was designed in 1942 as a cruiser tank to mount the new 17-pr gun. Prototypes were produced in the same year by the design firm, Birmingham Railway Carriage and Wagon Company, the use of many components of the Cromwell series easing many problems. Development of the turret was undertaken by Stothert and Pitt Ltd who were specialists in A.F.V. turret design. Problems were encountered during trials with the suspension and the turret and mounting, and then it was suggested that the 17-pr gun should be mounted in the Sherman, which was becoming available in increasing numbers to Britain.

The latter proved ultimately to be the best answer to the question of getting a powerful tank gun into the field where it could tackle the latest German tanks. Nevertheless, 200 Challengers were ordered and, the design snags eliminated, delivered during 1944. They were used chiefly by British regiments equipped with Cromwells in North West Europe, from Normandy onwards.

The illustrations show a tank of 8th King's Royal Irish Hussars, the armoured reconnaissance regiment of 7th Armoured Division.

25 Tank, Cruiser, Comet, U.K.

The Comet was the last of the line of British cruiser tanks and by far the best. It had a good gun and was fast and reliable.

Leyland Motors Limited undertook the design of the Comet: work was commenced during 1943 and the first prototype was completed in February 1944. Designed around the new 77-mm. gun—a shorter version of the 17-pr— some of the best features of the Cromwell were used, including the same Meteor engine. All-welded construction was used for the hull and turret, a system also employed with some of the later versions of the Cromwell. The Christie suspension system was again used but in a heavier form, since the Comet's weight was about 4½–5 tons heavier than that of the Cromwell.

After trials with the prototype, wider tracks were used and track return rollers (four each side) were added. A hull Besa machine-gun position like the Cromwell's was retained in the new design, and this was one point of subsequent criticism, because of the vertical plate it needed—far more vulnerable than the sloping glacis plate of the German Panther, one of the Comet's adversaries. The hull floor protection against mines was also felt to be not fully satisfactory.

The first production Comets arrived in September 1944 and, when delivered to armoured regiments towards the end of the year, met with general approval. The 77-mm. gun did not have quite the penetrative ability of the 17-pr but was very accurate and also had good high explosive ammunition. As a result of the German offensive in the Ardennes, which interrupted training, the Comet was not used in action until after the Rhine crossing in 1945. The first formation to be reequipped with the Comet was the 29th Armoured Brigade of 11th Armoured Division, and tanks of Regimental Headquarters, 2nd Fife and Forfar Yeomanry of this brigade are shown in the illustrations.

26 Tank, Cruiser, Ram and Armoured Personnel Carrier, Ram Kangaroo, Canada.

A cruiser tank designed and produced in Canada, the Ram foreshadowed some of the features of the U.S. Sherman Medium Tank, M.4.

Using the running gear of the U.S. M.3 Medium, the hull was completely redesigned in the light of British experience and the clumsy sponson of the M.3 was eliminated so that the main armament was concentrated in the turret. As only the 2-pr gun was available to start with, this was used in the prototype, which was running in June 1941. This gun (in an adapted Valentine mounting) also equipped the first fifty production vehicles to be built, and these were named Ram I. The turret design incorporated a removable front adapter plate, however, so that when the much more powerful 6-pr gun came along later, the turret was readily changed to accept this weapon. All the subsequent vehicles (of which 1,899 were built, production ending in 1943) had the 6-pr and were known as Ram II. The Ram (in both Marks) also carried two mounted 0·30-in. Browning machine-guns—one coaxial with the main armament and the second in the hull at the front left-hand side. On all the earlier vehicles this hull machine-gun was in a small auxiliary turret, although on the final vehicles to be built a ball and socket mounting was used instead. A further Browning machine-gun was carried for anti-aircraft use.

The engine used in the Ram tanks was the nine-cylinder radial Continental, developing 400 b.h.p.; the gearbox had five speeds and the steering was of the controlled differential type. With a top speed of 25 m.p.h., the Ram had maximum armour protection of 3 inches (76 mm.).

The Ram was used widely for training Canadian armoured units, but was never used in action as a battle tank, as the American Sherman became available in large quantities and was adopted more or less as the standard medium tank of the Allied Forces. However, when there was a call in 1944 for armoured personnel carriers to carry infantry into battle in the North West Europe campaign, the Ram chassis was used. Following earlier armoured personnel carriers, improvised for use in Normandy by the removal of the guns from Priest S.P.s (Priests and Shermans were also converted in Italy) the Ram Kangaroo became the standard British armoured personnel carrier. With the turret removed, the Ram could carry an infantry section of eight men, well protected by the hull armour, although lacking overhead cover. A British and a Canadian regiment were each equipped with Ram Kangaroos by December 1944 and, with a combined strength of 300 Kangaroos, operated under 79th Armoured Division until the end of the War.

The illustrations show a Ram II as used for training about 1942, and a Ram Kangaroo based on one of the later production vehicles with the hull ball m.g. mounting and no side doors.

27 **Australian Cruiser Tanks, Mark I and Mark III,** Australia.

The first pilot model of the first tank ever to be built in Australia was completed in January 1942. As World War II progressed, it became an increasing possibility that supplies of fighting vehicles from Britain or other Commonwealth countries for the Australian Army could not be counted on. Several hundreds of tracked carriers, based on designs adapted from drawings received from the United Kingdom were built in 1940–41, but when it was decided to undertake the production of cruiser tanks in Australia, it was felt preferable to develop an entirely new design consistent with Australian resources. The resulting design by Colonel W. D. Watson, a tank designer on loan to Australia from the United Kingdom, was entirely original.

The hull of the A.C.I. was cast in one piece—an unusual practice, but made necessary by the lack of capacity of Australian heavy industry to undertake the manufacture of the rolled plate, which it was originally intended to use in conjunction with smaller castings. A power unit of adequate performance was the next problem and, as no engine was available in Australia, or could be imported at that time, this was made up by combining three Cadillac V-8 cylinder petrol engines to form a 330 b.h.p. unit. These were at the rear of the hull in an arrangement of two beside each other, and the third centrally placed behind them. The power from all three engines was collected in a transfer box and thence forwards by one Carden shaft to the clutch and 5-speed crash gearbox. The track drive sprockets were at the front.

It had originally been the intention to adopt a suspension system, and tracks like those of the U.S. M.3 medium tanks but, although U.S. type tracks were used, the suspension finally chosen was the American type re-designed as a horizontal-volute spring type, resulting in a similar arrangement to that of the French Hotchkiss H-35 tank. The armament for the A.C.I had to be based on weapons of British design available in Australia, and this resulted in a turret-mounted 2-pr gun with coaxial 0·303-in. Vickers water-cooled machine-gun and another Vickers machine-gun centrally mounted in the front of the hull.

The armour was between 65 mm. and 25 mm. and, with an all-up weight of 28 tons, the A.C.I. had a top speed of 35 m.p.h. It was found to be not entirely reliable in service and, as by 1943 British and American tanks were available for Australia, no more than sixty-six A.C.I.s were built. In the meantime, however, improved Australian cruiser tanks were under development. As no heavier anti-tank gun than the 2-pr was to be had, the A.C.3 (the A.C.2 was a light cruiser design both started and abandoned in 1941) used the 25-pr field gun. A Vickers 0·303-in. machine-gun was mounted co-axially with the 25-pr. The hull machine-gun mounting of the A.C.I was omitted, the extra space being used for stowage of the larger 25-pr ammunition.

The Cadillac engine arrangement in the A.C.3 was improved and made more compact by their being mounted in a semi-radial pattern, so that all three engines were linked to a common crankcase.

The ultimate development of the A.C.I was the mounting of the 17-pr gun, this version to be known as A.C.4. After recoil tests with twin 25-pr guns in a special turret on an A.C.I, the 17-pr gun then produced in Australia was mounted successfully. Around 700 tanks of the A.C.3 and A.C.4 types were needed by the Australian Army, but apart from the experimental models none of these were built, because of the change in priorities in

Australian war production brought about by supplies of A.F.V.s from overseas. The A.C.1s built were, however, used by the Australian Army for many years for defence, and then training, the last of them being declared obsolete in 1956.

28 Tanks, Infantry, Mark IV, Churchill III and Churchill VII, U.K.

The first versions of the Infantry Tank Mark IV, to appear in 1941—the Churchills I and II—were equipped, of necessity, with 2-pr gun turrets. However, as a supply of 6-pr guns became available the Churchill III entered the production line, using a welded turret designed by Babcock and Wilcox Limited. Mechanically the same as its predecessors, having the 350-h.p. Bedford twelve-cylinder with a Merritt-Brown 4-speed gearbox, the Churchill III differed from the Churchill I–III mainly in the different turret and ammunition stowage. A little later, the Churchill III was joined on the production lines by a further version, Churchill IV, with the same armament but having a cast instead of a welded turret.

At the earliest opportunity, earlier marks of Churchill were reworked and had their 2-pr turrets replaced by new turrets with the 6-pr gun.

The Dieppe Raid in August 1942 was used to try out the Churchill in action for the first time. Some thirty Churchill tanks, mostly Churchill IIIs, but with a handful of Churchill Is and IIs (the latter equipped with flamethrowers), were used in support but had little

chance of proving themselves, as few were able to surmount the sea wall and penetrate inland.

Some Churchill IIIs and other Marks were among the tanks supplied to the U.S.S.R. in 1942, but it was not until the Tunisian campaign of 1942–43 that the Churchill, represented mainly by Mark IIIs and IVs, really proved its worth, particularly in mountainous country.

Development in the meantime resulted in the Churchill V, a close support version equipped with a 95-mm. howitzer and the Churchill VI, similar to the Churchill IV but with a British-built 75-mm. gun in place of the 6-pr.

An entirely new version of the Churchill was designed by Vauxhall Motors Limited, the original 'parent' company for the group of Churchill tank manufacturers, to meet a new War Office specification A.22F (later renumbered A.42) for an infantry tank with 6-in. frontal armour. The new model, known as Churchill VII, although superficially similar to earlier Churchills, used a completely different form of hull construction in that a hull frame was dispensed with, the armour plate itself forming the hull. Many detailed improvements were incorporated, the most obvious being circular side doors and driver's vision port instead of the rectangular variety. A commander's turret vision cupola was introduced after the first few Churchill VIIs were built. The Churchill VII had main armament of a 75-mm. gun with a coaxial 7·92-mm. Besa machine-gun and another Besa in the hull front. A close support tank, Churchill VIII, was identical except for the 95-mm. howitzer which replaced the 75-mm. gun.

A ton heavier than earlier models, Churchills VII and VIII had a heavier suspension system and slightly lower ratios in the gearbox, and the governed top speed was reduced from about 16 m.p.h. to about 13 m.p.h.

Reliable, with heavy armour and a reasonably satisfactory gun, the Churchill VII (together with earlier models brought up to roughly the same standard) was one of the most important British tanks in both the Italian and North West Europe campaigns until the end of the war, during which 5,640 of all Marks were built.

The illustrations show a Churchill III of 142nd (Suffolk) Regiment, Royal Armoured Corps, at the time of the Tunisian campaign, and a Churchill VII in the colours of 6th (Guards) Tank Brigade.

29 S.P. 25-pr, Bishop and S.P. 17-pr, Archer, U.K.

The war in the North African desert emphasized the need for both increased mobility and protection for field and anti-tank artillery. The Bishop was designed hurriedly in 1941 in response to an urgent request from the Middle East for a self-propelled mounting for the 25-pr field gun—a weapon that had often been found to be the only effective answer to the German medium tanks. Designed by the Birmingham Railway Carriage and Wagon Company Limited, the sturdy and reliable Valentine tank chassis was used as the carrier for the 25-pr gun, which was mounted in a fixed shield with a total

traverse of 8 degrees, elevation of 15 degrees and depression of 5 degrees.

One hundred Bishops were built by July 1942, and nearly all of them were used in the North African campaigns.

As a design to meet an emergency, the Bishop served its purpose but was never entirely satisfactory and, although some continued in action in Sicily and Italy in 1943, it was replaced as soon as possible by the U.S.-built Priest S.P. 105-mm. or the Canadian Sexton S.P. 25-pr.

The Bishop design was proposed as the basis of a self-propelled mounting for the new 17-pr anti-tank gun in 1942, but this was found to be impracticable. Nevertheless, the Valentine chassis was again used but this time with a rearward-facing layout for the gun. Two prototypes were completed in the first part of 1943 by Vickers-Armstrongs. After some modifications to the gun traverse system, frontal armour and other features, production began: the first vehicles were delivered in 1944, and a total of 665 of them were finished by the end of the war.

The rear-facing arrangement of the 17-pr gun in the Archer permitted a compact design—particularly useful in an anti-tank gun—and a total traverse of 45 degrees allowed reasonable flexibility in use. The welded upper hull had armour protection up to 20 mm.—effective against small arms. A 0·30-in. Browning machine-gun was carried for protection against local ground attack and aircraft.

The Bishop used the Valentine II chassis with an A.E.C. 131 b.h.p. diesel engine, but the Archer chassis was equivalent to that of the later models of Valentine tank with the

General Motors diesel of 192 b.h.p., giving a top speed of 20 m.p.h.—compared with the slightly heavier Bishop's 15 m.p.h.

Although the merits (rapid withdrawal in emergency, for one) and demerits of the rearward-facing gun were often debated, the Archer was generally acknowledged as reliable and the effectiveness of the 17-pr gun was never in doubt. The Archer was used by anti-tank regiments in North West Europe and Italy from 1944 onwards, and continued to be employed by the British Army for several years after the war. An Archer of the anti-tank regiment of 15th (Scottish) Division in Germany in 1945 is shown in the illustration. The Bishop shown is as it appeared in the Sicily campaign in 1943.

30 S.P.25-pr Sexton, Canada.

The Sexton was probably the most important Canadian-built tracked vehicle to be used in action—it was the principal self-propelled field artillery piece employed by British and Canadian armoured formations in 1944–45.

Based on the chassis of the Canadian Ram cruiser tank (which never saw combat as a battle tank) the Sexton was designed by the Canadian Army Engineering Design Branch. Intended as a replacement in the Commonwealth Armies for the U.S. M.7 Priest S.P. 105-mm., the Sexton was not unlike the M.7 in appearance, and the suspension of both vehicles shared a common ancestry with the U.S. M.3 Medium tank.

The British 25-pr field gun was mounted slightly to the left of centre in an open-top welded armoured superstructure, where it had a traverse of 25 degrees left and 15 degrees right, and an elevation of 40 degrees. Eighty-seven high explosive and smoke shells were carried together with eighteen armour-piercing shells for anti-tank use. Two 0·303-in. Bren machine-guns were carried (but not normally mounted) for local protection, although in some vehicles a 0·50-in. Browning heavy machine-gun was mounted at the front of the hull at the left.

The nine-cylinder Continental engine of 400 b.h.p. (484 b.h.p. in later models), used in the Ram and in some models of the U.S. M.3 and M.4 medium tanks, in the Sexton gave a top speed of 25 m.p.h.

Production of the Sexton took place at the Montreal Locomotive Works Tank Arsenal, and a total of 2,150 of them was completed by the end of World War II.

The illustrations show (top) a Sexton belonging to the 5th Royal Horse Artillery (7th Armoured Division) and (below) to the 147th (Essex Yeomanry) Field Regiment, Royal Artillery (8th Armoured Brigade), both operating in the North West Europe campaign.

31 Sherman D.D., U.K.

One of the most ingenious, yet basically simple, devices of World War II was Nicholas Straussler's D.D. amphibious tank. By water-proofing the hull and raising the freeboard, it was found that an ordinary tank could be made to float without the necessity for the clumsy buoyancy chambers or pontoons, or a boat type of hull as used in earlier amphibious tanks. The means used by Straussler to increase the freeboard was to add a canvas screen around the edge of the hull. Tried out first on a 7½-ton Light Tank Mark VII in 1941, the screen was raised by means of inflatable rubber tubes and held erect by metal struts. Production of 625 D.D. tanks based on the 17-ton Valentine tank then took place and deliveries were made in 1943–44. It was, however, desired to extend the use of the D.D. device to the Sherman, virtually the standard medium tank used by the British Army, and Sherman D.D. prototypes were built and proved as successful as the earlier models, although the 30-ton tank needed higher screens to produce the buoyancy required to make it float.

As in earlier D.D. tanks, the Sherman had Duplex Drive (hence the initials)—normal propulsion on tracks on land and propellers for movement on water. The tracks of the Sherman were also run in water because the power take off to drive the twin 3-bladed propellers was implemented through stub axles on the rear idler wheels. The propellers were movable for steering, which was operated by the tank commander through either mechanical linkage to the propellers or a hydraulic system.

The water speed of the Sherman D.D. was up to 6 m.p.h. and, as the tracks were running all the time the tank was afloat, it could climb ashore the moment it touched ground. The screens could be lowered quickly, and the Sherman's armament, a 75-mm. gun and 0·30-in. Browning in the turret (the hull machine-gun had had to be eliminated in the D.D.) could then be used.

A tactical surprise was achieved with the first use of Sherman D.D. tanks in action on some Normandy beaches in 1944, because in the water they were not immediately recognized as tanks. They were also used later on in the Italian campaign (together with a small number of Valentine D.D.s) and at the Rhine crossing in March 1945.

The illustrations show a Sherman D.D. (with screens folded) of 4th Armoured Brigade in Germany in 1945, a Sherman D.D. afloat, and one on land with the screens raised.

32 Churchill VII Crocodile and Grant C.D.L., U.K.

The first British tank-borne flamethrower to be sent into action was the Churchill Oke. Three Churchill IIs with this hastily produced flamethrower equipment were among the tanks used in the raid on Dieppe in August 1942 but, as it happened, the landing craft carrying all three never reached the beach, being sunk offshore.

A more satisfactory design of tank flamethrower was already in hand and twelve pilot models were ordered by the War Office at the end of July 1942. Mounted in the Churchill IV, the flamethrowers were of the Wasp type already used successfully in Carriers. The fuel for the flame projector, which replaced the hull machine-gun, was carried in an armoured trailer and was pumped through under pressure obtained from compressed gas cylinders. A range of between 100 and 200 yards was attainable. One thousand Crocodile equipments were ordered and some 800 were completed by the end of the war. The Churchill VII was used as the basis of the production Crocodiles and a rectangular hatch in the hull floor for the mounting of the flame equipment was included as standard in all Churchill VIIs and VIIIs, so that they could readily be adapted for this role. Apart from the hull machine-gun, all the rest of the normal Churchill VIIs armament was carried in the Crocodile.

Crocodiles equipped a tank brigade in the North West Europe campaign and were also used in smaller numbers in Italy. A Churchill VII Crocodile of C Squadron, 51st Royal Tank Regiment in the latter theatre of war is shown in the illustration.

Another form of special armour used in the North West Europe campaign, the development of which began several years earlier, was the C.D.L. tank. The initials stood for Canal Defence Light—a deliberately misleading code name, since by dazzling enemy gunners the tank was intended to support attacks. The device consisted of a high intensity arc lamp, the beam of which was, by reflectors, projected through a vertical slit in the armoured face of the special turret. The dazzle effect could be enhanced by operating a shutter, causing the beam to flicker.

Originally fitted to Matilda infantry tanks, and used on training in the United Kingdom and the Middle East, the C.D.L. was later standardized on the U.S.-built Grant. The advantage in using this tank was that the main armament of a 75-mm. gun in the hull sponson could be retained, only the small 37-mm. gun turret having to be removed to fit the C.D.L. turret.

Because of the wish to keep this weapon secret for an important action in which it could be used to the best effect—and perhaps because of ignorance of its potential (or existence) by senior commanders—the C.D.L. was not used in action until nearly the end of the war, at the Rhine and Elbe river crossings. Even so they seem to have been used as little more than ordinary static searchlights, rather than in a true assault function.

The Grant C.D.L. tanks, like the Crocodiles, in North West Europe came under the aegis of 79th Armoured Division, and one belonging to that formation is shown here.

33 Matilda Scorpion and Grant Scorpion, U.K.

The most effective device for clearing minefields devised in World War II, the flail tank, was the idea of Major A. S. J. du Toit, a motor engineer serving with the South African Union Defence Force. A working model to demonstrate the idea was built, and details were given to the Middle East Mechanical Experimental Establishment, before Major du Toit was despatched to the United Kingdom where better resources for development of the device were available.

The anti-mine flail was a power-driven revolving drum to which rows of heavy chains were attached which, beating the ground in front of the vehicle to which the device was fitted, exploded mines on contact.

The Mechanical Experimental Establishment in the Middle East first fitted the device to a lorry and then, after trials, to a Matilda tank. This equipment was then called Matilda Scorpion Mark I.

The flails of the Matilda Scorpion I were made up of wire cable to the ends of which short lengths of chain were attached. The rotating drum was driven by a Ford V-8 engine, mounted in an armoured box on the right-hand side of the tank's hull. A cardan shaft took the transmission along the supporting girder to a bevel box and from it to the rotor. The flail engine was operated by an extra crew member who had the unenviable job of sitting at the rear of the armoured box behind the engine. In this position he was nearly choked by dust and fumes from the flail engine.

An order for twenty-four Matilda Scorpion Mark Is was completed in time for them to be used to help clear minefields for the Battle of Alamein in October 1942. Still beset by mechanical difficulties and with a flailing speed of only ½ m.p.h., nevertheless the Scorpions were considered reasonably satisfactory. A better version in which the flail operator was carried in the tank itself, and the design of the side girder was changed and other improvements effected, was known as the Matilda Scorpion Mark II and was ready by early 1943.

In order to take advantage of the greater mobility of the American Grant, the Scorpion Mark II flail equipment was adapted to this tank, the combination being known as Grant Scorpion Mark III. The hull-mounted 75-mm. gun had to be removed, but the 37-mm. gun turret could be retained although this was also, in fact, removed when it was necessary to reduce the overall dimensions to be carried in landing craft. Grant Scor-

pions were used in the Sicily campaign in the summer of 1943.

The final developments of the flail tank which took place in the Middle East, parallel to work in the same field in the United Kingdom, were the Grant Scorpion IV and the Sherman Scorpion. The former used two Dodge engines, mounted at the rear of the hull, driving the rotating drum by means of cardan shafts each side. This equipment was used in very similar form on the Sherman tank, and Sherman Scorpions in small numbers were used in the Italian campaign.

A Matilda Scorpion Mark I and a Grant Scorpion Mark IV are shown in the illustrations.

34 Sherman Crab I and Crab II, U.K.

From the end of 1941 onwards development of the flail tank, initiated by Major A. S. J. du Toit, took place at the works of A.E.C. Ltd in the United Kingdom. At first undertaken independently of the parallel experiments in the Middle East, later on ideas were exchanged. The best design of flail tank to enter service in World War II, the Sherman Crab incorporated ideas from both centres of development.

The first U.K. flail tank, known as Baron, used the Matilda chassis. Early models had one engine to drive the flail but the final model had two flail engines. Sixty were built in 1943 for training purposes. The next type, the Valentine Scorpion, was based on designs received from the Middle East, although the rotor was like that of the Baron. Again, only a small order

(150 vehicles) for training only was given.

Next, flail development was transferred to the Sherman tank—this had the advantage of using the same basic vehicle that was to equip many British armoured regiments.

Prototypes of three models were built in 1943, the Sherman Marquis, turretless and based on the Baron and Scorpion; the Sherman Pram Scorpion, retaining its turret and taking its flail drive from the tank's main engines; and the Sherman Crab. The latter was considered to be the best design and was the one adopted for production in quantity for employment in the forthcoming campaign in North West Europe.

Fitted to the Sherman V, powered by a Chrysler thirty-cylinder 350 b.h.p. engine, the flail was operated through a power take off on the right-hand side of the hull, leading through a universal-jointed cardan shaft to a bevel gear at the rotor. The rotor arms could be lifted by hydraulic rams to make transport in landing craft etc. easier. A lane 9 ft 9 in. wide could be cleared of mines at a maximum speed of 1¼ m.p.h. Six hundred and eighty-nine Crabs were ordered and were widely used throughout the North West Europe campaign in 1944–45, where they operated under the command of 79th Armoured Division.

A later model, Sherman Crab II (which did not become available until nearly the end of the war) was developed to overcome the fault of Crab I and all other earlier flail tanks, in that mines buried in hollows in the ground could be passed over without being detonated because the flails operated at a constant height above a level surface. The left hand hydraulic lifting ram was replaced by a counter weight attached to the rear end of the rotor arm. This enabled the rotor arm and bearing chains to maintain a constant height over the contours of the ground.

The illustrations show a Sherman Crab I with the rotor arm at beating height (attachments on the rear of the hull are station-keeping-lights—for the benefit of following vehicles—mounted above the box containing markers to indicate the swept lane) and a Sherman Crab II flailing in a depression in the ground.

35 Churchill A.V.R.E. Carpet-layer and S.B.G. Bridge Carrier, U.K.

The Dieppe Raid of 1942, in which heavy losses were sustained by both armour and infantry, chiefly because the tanks were unable to penetrate inland, indicated the need for protection for engineers working to surmount or destroy obstacles. A suggestion by Lieutenant J. J. Denovan, of the Royal Canadian Engineers, that a tank should be adapted for this purpose was followed up by the R.C.E. using a Churchill tank. The Churchill was chosen because it had a well-armoured, roomy hull. It also had a relatively large door on each side of the hull, suitable for use by sappers under fire and for loading stores and equipment. The prototype with rearranged stowage was ready by December 1942 and a spigot motor, developed separately, was ready by February 1943 and mounted in the modified turret. The spigot motor, known as Petard, could throw a 40-lb projectile (containing a 26-lb charge) up to an extreme range of 230 yards, and was capable of destroying concrete obstacles.

The Assault Vehicle, Royal Engineers, or A.V.R.E. as it was usually called, was adjudged successful after trials and modifications to the original design which took place in 1943, and production was ordered. The Churchill III or IV was used as the basis, and a total of about 700 A.V.R.E.s was built by 1945.

Most production A.V.R.E.s were fitted with brackets on the hull for the attachment of fittings for special tasks. One of these fitments was the carpet-layer device for crossing soft patches on beaches, for example. The carpet—the most common form was hessian matting reinforced by steel tubes—was carried on a large bobbin at the front of the A.V.R.E. and was unwound by the vehicle itself running over it. A number of these were employed on the D-Day landing beaches, There were several versions, and the Carpetlayer Type D (waterproofed for landing from a landing craft) is shown in the illustration.

Another important use of the A.V.R.E. was as a carrier for the Small Box Girder (S.B.G.) bridge, which could carry a 40-ton load (the weight of a Churchill tank) over a 30-ft span. This could be laid mechanically under fire.

The A.V.R.E. was used in action in Italy and in North West Europe. Three Assault Regiments, Royal Engineers, under the command of 79th Armoured Division, with A.V.R.E.s and a variety of fitments, took part in many actions from D-Day onwards. An A.V.R.E. with S.B.G. bridge as it appeared in the attack on the Le Havre fortifications is illustrated.

36 Churchill A.R.V., Mark I and Sherman B.A.R.V., U.K.

The weakness of the British organization for the recovery of disabled tanks was brought out particularly in the early campaigns in the North African desert, where the Germans proved to be well in advance in this respect.

Early in 1942, a Royal Electrical and Mechanical Engineers experimental section undertook the design of armoured recovery vehicles on tank chassis. The idea was to use adaptations as A.R.V.s of the same kinds of tanks used by the armoured regiments, in so far as the basic chassis was suitable for use also as a recovery vehicle. The three most important A.R.V. types which emerged were based on the Cromwell, Sherman and Churchill, corresponding with the principal tanks in use from 1943 onwards.

The Churchill A.R.V., Mark I, was a turretless vehicle carrying a 3-ton jib. This was stowed on the hull for travelling but was mounted between the front 'horns' when in use and was capable of lifting out tank engines or other major assemblies for maintenance and repair. A 100-ft length of heavy steel cable was carried for hauling out bogged-down A.F.V.s and a pulley block and ground anchors were available for indirect or difficult recovery jobs. The A.R.V. also carried a 4½-in. vice and oxy-acetylene and welding plant among its equipment. Sherman and Cromwell A.R.V.s, Mark I, were also built and had similar equipment to the Churchill A.R.V.

Mark II versions of the Churchill and Sherman A.R.V.s were also produced and began to become available in 1944. These had fixed turrets with dummy guns: a fixed jib (with a 9½-ton lift) was carried at the rear and a demountable 3½-ton jib at the front. Other improved equipment included a 60-ton-pull-winch, the operator of which sat in the turret.

Development of an A.R.V. to recover disabled tanks or vehicles, both in the water and on the beaches, was commenced in 1943 specially for the forthcoming invasion of Europe. Churchill and Sherman tanks were tested in this role, but the former was abandoned because of the far greater amount of waterproofing it needed. The diesel-engined Sherman III was finally selected as the standard chassis for the Beach Armoured Recovery Vehicle (B.A.R.V.). Fully waterproofed and able to operate in up to 10 feet of water, the Sherman B.A.R.V. was intended only for simple recovery operations, such as towing vehicles 'drowned' in landing from landing craft or pushing off stranded landing craft, for which wooden railway sleepers mounted on the front were provided.

The Sherman B.A.R.V.s well served their purpose in 1944 by helping to keep the D-Day beaches clear. One B.A.R.V. was inadvertently the cause of more direct alarm to the enemy because, landed in error at a very early stage of the invasion, it was taken to be a new 'secret weapon'.

The illustrations show a Churchill A.R.V., Mark I, belonging to the 3rd (Tank) Battalion Scots Guards, and a standard Sherman B.A.R.V.

37 Carrier, Universal, Mark II, and Carrier, 2-pr, Tank Attack (Aust.), U.K. and Australia.

The British Army's demand for tracked carriers of the Bren and Scout types, and for a variety of functions, remained high throughout World War II, but even by 1940 the need was felt to standardize the design as far as possible. This resulted in the introduction of the Carrier, Universal. Mechanically the same as the earlier carriers, the Universal was powered by a Ford V-8 engine which drove the tracks via rear sprockets. Steering was by lateral displacement of the front bogie unit for gentle turns, with track braking for more abrupt turns. Although the driver's and gunner's compartments were very much the same in all carriers, the position of the armoured rear compartment varied. In the Universal Carrier, the whole of the rear was armoured, providing an open-top compartment on either side of the engine.

As before, both British and imported Ford V-8 engines were used in the Universal Carrier, and the final list of these was as follows:

No. 1　　　British-built engine.
No. 2 and 2a American-built engines—
　　　　　models　G.A.E.　and
　　　　　G.A.E.A. respectively.
No. 3　　　Canadian-built engine.
The British-built engines were originally rated at 65 b.h.p., the American engines at 85 b.h.p. and the Canadian

ones at 95 b.h.p., although at the end of the war the War Office rated them all at 85 b.h.p. In any event, engines from all three sources were inter-changeable.

The Mark II version of the Universal Carrier included some improvements, such as a spare road wheel as a standard fitting, a larger kit box on the rear of the hull, and either one or two foot-step brackets each side of the hull. Some further improvements were incorporated in the Mark III Carrier. There were also other carriers such as Carriers M.M.G., Mortar, and Armoured Observation Post, but these had basically the same hull form as the Universal Carrier, with only relatively minor adaptations to fit their specialized roles.

Some 40,000 or more Carriers of the Universal and later associated types were built in the United Kingdom alone during World War II but, even so, it was felt necessary that Commonwealth countries should also undertake the production of tracked carriers. In Canada 29,000 of the Universal-type were built to a similar specification to the U.K. version (about 5,000 of the larger Windsor carriers were also built in Canada and the U.S.A. produced 14,000 T.16 series Carriers). A Carrier, Universal, Mark II, belonging to an infantry battalion of 43rd (Wessex) Division is illustrated.

In Australia and New Zealand carriers were also built. The earliest N.Z. carriers were built from plans sent from the United Kingdom, although later models were more like the Australian ones. Australian production was much greater, to meet the heavier demand in that country, and the basic U.K. carrier design was simplified

mechanically in that the track displacement device for steering was omitted. Although in other respects broadly the same as the U.K. carriers, the later Australian carriers had a modified hull with a sloping glacis plate. Also, welded construction was used—a feature employed only in some models of the U.K.-built carriers.

In 1942 an experimental version of the Australian carrier with a stronger, lengthened chassis was built as a mounting for the 2-pr anti-tank gun. The Ford V-8 engine was brought forward alongside the driver and the gun, on a field mounting with shield, was on a turntable at the rear. Trials of the 2-pr carrier showed various faults; among others it rode badly, was slow and underpowered; was insufficiently strong and mechanical components failed; the driver was too cramped and the crew and gun were inadequately protected. It did not, therefore, go into series production, although the 5,600 standard Universal-type Carriers built in Australia gave useful service.

38 **South African Armoured Reconnaissance Cars, Mark IV and Mark VI,** South Africa.

Experience with the South African Reconnaissance Car, Mark II, on active service in East Africa and Libya in 1940–41, showed the need for further improvements and some of these were incorporated in the next model, Mark III, also using a Ford Marmon-Herrington chassis. However, neither model was armed with an anti-tank gun, and as a temporary expedient armoured car regiments often fitted heavier weapons of calibres of 20 mm. upwards, taken from captured enemy A.F.V.s or derelict British tanks.

Consequently, it was decided to build the next model to take a 2-pr gun. This vehicle, the South African Armoured Reconnaissance Car, Mark IV, once again used Marmon-Herrington automotive components but it was a complete redesign, in which the welded armoured hull acted as the chassis to which the engine, suspension, etc., were attached directly. A rear-engine layout was adopted, with the driver at the front and a central fighting compartment. Of fairly light construction, it was felt that the turret could not absorb the recoil of a tank-pattern 2-pr gun and so a 2-pr field mounting was used, with the prominent recuperator under the barrel. A coaxial 0·30-in. Browning machine-gun was added in the final standard form of the Mark IV, together with a 0·50-in. or (more usually) a 0·30-in. Browning on an anti-aircraft mount on the turret roof.

There was a strong demand for South African-built armoured cars from the War Office, as well as the Union Defence Force and, as the supply of components from Marmon-Herrington in the U.S.A. seemed unlikely to meet requirements, the design of the Mark IV was modified to employ instead automotive components from Canadian Ford F 60L 3-ton, 4-wheel drive lorries. These lorries were diverted to South Africa from War Office orders for the Middle East Forces. The Canadian F 60Ls already incorporated driven front axles of Marmon-Herrington design, so they could readily be used. The resulting vehicle was known as South African Armoured Reconnaissance Car,

Mark IV F (the 'F' probably denoting the Ford connection). In British War Office nomenclature, the two types were known as 'Armoured Car, Marmon-Herrington'—Mark IV and Mark IV F.

A total of 2,116 Mark IV and Mark IV F cars was built and, although they were used for defence in South Africa and were issued to the Arab Legion and some Allied Forces, none were received in time to be used in combat in North Africa. The same fate applied to the much larger South African Armoured Reconnaissance Car, Mark VI.

The Mark VI resulted from the strong impression created by the German eight-wheeled armoured cars, which proved to be well suited to desert conditions. Again, the well-proven Ford Marmon-Herrington components were used, this time two sets with two engines, each of 95 b.h.p. Armament and, to a degree, armour was to be of cruiser tank standard, and consisted of a 2-pr gun and a coaxial 0·30-in. Browning machine-gun, with 30-mm. maximum protection. There was also a turret ring mounting with two 0·30-in. Browning machine-guns for anti-aircraft use. The second prototype was armed with a 6-pr gun and coaxial 7·92-mm. Besa machine-gun, with a 0·50-in. Browning anti-aircraft machine-gun.

By the time that production of the Mark VI could commence—delayed as it was by a shortage of components in South Africa—the North African campaign was well-nigh over. Armoured cars from other sources were becoming available in better quantities and, as the Mark VI was considered less well suited to the European terrain, the production orders were cancelled.

The illustrations show a standard S.A. Armoured Reconnaissance Car, Mark IV, and the first prototype S.A. Armoured Reconnaissance Car, Mark VI—operating during trials before the anti-aircraft ring mounting was fitted.

39 **Armoured Cars, Humber, Mark III and Mark IV,** U.K.

Humber Armoured Cars were numerically the most important British-built armoured cars of World War II, well over 5,000 being produced by the Rootes Group between 1940 and 1945.

The earliest Humber Armoured Car, the Mark I, was almost identical externally to the Guy Mark IA Armoured Car, and its mechanical layout although based, of course, on Rootes components was on similar lines to that of the Guy. Service experience suggested improvements and a cleaned-up front end, incorporating the driver's visor in the glacis plate, and radiator intake improvements were introduced in the Mark II.

The Armoured Car, Humber Mark III, which entered production in 1942 had a more roomy turret than the Marks I–II, which allowed the crew to be increased to four. The first three Marks of Humber Armoured Car all had an armament of two Besa machine-guns, one of 7·92-mm. calibre and the other 15-mm. The latter was never an entirely satisfactory weapon, being prone to stoppages, and in the Humber Mark IV Armoured Car the American 37-mm. gun was introduced in its place. Because this reduced the turret

space available, the crew was reduced to three men.

All the Humber Armoured Cars weighed about 7 tons and their 90-b.h.p. six-cylinder engines gave them a top speed of 45 m.p.h. They were used by both armoured car regiments (where they tended to be used at regimental and squadron headquarters if Daimlers were also available) and Reconnaissance Regiments (of infantry divisions) in most theatres of war in which British and Commonwealth troops were engaged up to the end of the war. The illustrations show a Mark III as it appeared in the North African desert about 1942, and a Mark IV of 1st Reconnaissance Regiment in Italy in 1944.

40 **Armoured Cars, Daimler, Mark I and Mark II,** U.K.

Inspired to a large extent by the design of the Car, Scout Mark I, the Daimler Armoured Car was built to the 'Tank, Light, Wheeled' formula of a wheeled vehicle having performance, armour and armament comparable to that of contemporary light tanks. After some initial difficulties it turned out to be one of the best armoured cars of World War II.

The mechanical layout of the Daimler Armoured Car consisted of a rear-mounted, 95 b.h.p. six-cylinder engine from which the transmission was taken via a 'Fluid Flywheel' and pre-selector gearbox to a centrally mounted transfer box with a single differential. From this the power was transmitted via four parallel driving shafts and Tracta universal joints to each wheel, with final reduction gears in each hub. This arrangement helped to keep the height down, as there were no central transmission shafts, and a further point making for compact design was that all the automotive components were attached direct to the hull, there being no chassis as such. Although regarded as being somewhat underpowered, the Daimler Armoured Car had a good cross-country performance and a top road speed of 50 m.p.h. Two other interesting features were the early use of disc brakes, and the inclusion of a second steering wheel facing the rear, together with basic driving controls, to enable the car to be driven rapidly in reverse in emergency.

The armament of the Daimler Armoured Car was identical to that of the Tetrarch Light Tank (with which it shared the turret design), a 2-pr gun and coaxially mounted 7·92-mm. Besa machine-gun.

Some improvements suggested by experience in service of the Daimler Mark I were incorporated in the Mark II, which followed the Mark I into production towards the latter end of the war. The most important changes were a 2-speed dynamo, a driver's escape hatch in the hull roof, an improved gun mantlet, and a different radiator and grill. Both Marks of Daimler (a total of 2,694 of which was built) sometimes had Littlejohn Adaptors added to the 2-pr guns, which greatly increased their penetrative ability.

The Daimler Mark I Armoured Car was first used in action in North Africa in 1942, and subsequently with the Mark II in Europe and the Far East. Many British and Commonwealth armoured car regiments used these cars and the illustrations show a Mark I of the 1st Derbyshire Yeomanry (6th Armoured Division) in Tunisia, and a Mark II of 11th Hussars (7th Armoured Division) in Germany in 1945.

41 Armoured Cars, A.E.C., Mark II and Mark III, U.K.

The original A.E.C. Armoured Car (Mark I) was conceived by the Associated Equipment Company Limited in 1941 as a heavy armoured car with both armour and armament equivalent to that of a cruiser tank and, in fact, used the 2-pr turret of a Valentine tank. This private venture was successful and 122 of them were built, many being sent to North Africa in 1942. When British tank armament increased, the A.E.C. Mark II Armoured Car was designed to use the 6-pr gun (with a coaxial 7·92-mm. Besa machine-gun) and, at the same time, the opportunity was taken to redesign the shape of the front hull and introduce other improvements. The Mark II had a more powerful A.E.C. diesel engine of 158 b.h.p. (which gave a top speed of 41 m.p.h.) and a crew of four. It weighed 12·7 tons and the armour protection was at a maximum of 30 mm.

The next step, in the Mark III, was to substitute the British 75-mm. gun for the 6-pr. The Mark III was very similar to its predecessor in most other respects, except that it had two (rather than one) electric fans installed in the turret roof. A total of 507 Armoured Cars, A.E.C. Marks II and III was built.

Some A.E.C. Mark IIs were supplied to the Yugoslav partisans in 1944 and one of these is shown in the smaller illustration. A.E.C. Mark IIIs were used principally in the Heavy Troops of British Armoured Car Regiments in the North West Europe campaign, and a car of 2nd Household Cavalry Regiment (then in VIII Corps) is illustrated.

42 Car, Scout, Humber, Mark I, U.K.

Production of the Daimler Scout Car (introduced into service at the beginning of World War II) was continued throughout the war. Only relatively minor changes were made in the design because it was a highly successful vehicle. However, as the number built could not meet the demand, the Rootes Group was asked to design and manufacture a scout car to supplement the Daimler Scout Cars.

To avoid unnecessary production complications the Rootes Group design which became known as Car, Scout, Humber, Mark I, employed a high proportion of components used in existing Humber 4-wheel drive military vehicles, such as the Light Reconnaissance Car, but adapted for a rear engine layout. The ubiquitous Rootes 87 b.h.p. six-cylinder engine was linked to a 4-speed gearbox and gave a top speed of 60 m.p.h. Rather larger than the Daimler Scout Car and with room for three men, the Humber Scout Car was of a mechanically less sophisticated design, and the maximum frontal protection was only 14 mm. compared with the Daimler's 30 mm. For some or all of these reasons, given a choice, armoured regiments tended to use

Humbers for liaison purposes rather than scouting.

The Mark II version of the Humber Scout Car was externally similar to the Mark I but had synchromesh added to 2nd gear as well as in 3rd and 4th. A total of 4,300 Humber Scout Cars was built between about late 1942 and the end of the war.

The illustrations show vehicles belonging to 11th Armoured Division.

43 Car, Scout, Ford, Lynx I–II, and Car, Light Reconnaissance, Canadian G.M., Mark I, Otter I, Canada.

As well as manufacturing large numbers of tanks, Canadian industry made a significant contribution to the production of wheeled armoured vehicles for the Commonwealth during World War II. Many chassis were supplied for armoured vehicles built in India and South Africa, but among the most important produced complete in Canada itself were the Lynx Scout Car and the Otter Light Reconnaissance Car—products of Ford and General Motors respectively.

The drawings of the Daimler Scout Car were sent from the United Kingdom to Canada so that an equivalent vehicle could be built to supplement British production, which lagged behind demand. It would have been impracticable to undertake the extensive re-tooling and conversion of standard measurements that would have been needed to produce a replica of the Daimler Scout Car in Canada, so the Daimler's hull design was adapted to accept a Ford V-8 engine and Ford 4-

wheel drive automative components. As the Ford transmission was of the conventional pattern for 4-wheel drive vehicles, with centrally placed transmission shafts to front and rear axles, the Canadian Scout Car was of necessity nearly a foot taller than the Daimler.

Known originally in British nomenclature simply as Car, Scout, Mark III (and later as Lynx I) the early versions of this car were found to be unreliable and some components needed strengthening. Later vehicles were modified in various ways, including a revision of the radiator protection at the rear. A second model, known as Car, Scout, Ford Mark II, Lynx II, incorporated the results of both production experience with Lynx I and British operating experience with Scout cars generally, which led to the omission of the armoured roof, which was rarely used. The Lynx II was considered to be reliable and had a better performance than its predecessor. The chief external difference (apart from the roof) was the sand channels carried at the rear in the Lynx II, instead of across the front locker.

A Lynx II is shown in the illustration.

The Ford V-8 95 b.h.p. engine in the Lynx Scout cars gave a top speed of between 55 and 60 m.p.h. and the armour protection, like that of the Daimler Scout cars, was at a maximum of 30 mm. on the sloping glacis plate.

A total of 3,255 Lynx I and II Scout cars was built. They were used by the Canadian Army in Italy and North West Europe, and by British and Indian troops in the Far East.

The Canadian-built Car, Light Reconnaissance, Canadian G.M. Mark I,

Otter I was built to the same general specification as the British Humber Mark III Light Reconnaissance Car. The use of Canadian components, however, resulted in a shorter bonnet and a higher, more humped hull, although provision was made for the same armament—a Bren 0·303-in. machine-gun in the turret and a 0·55-in. Boys anti-tank rifle in the hull front beside the driver. Alternatively, a No. 19 wireless set was carried in the latter position. The six-cylinder General Motors engine developed 104 b.h.p., and gave a maximum speed of 45 m.p.h. The crew of three were protected by armour varying between 12 mm. and 6 mm.

Although of less good performance than the Humber Light Reconnaissance Car (mainly because it was over a ton heavier and lacked an auxiliary gearbox) the 1761 Otters built gave useful service in all the main theatres of war with the Canadian and British Armies (and, in addition, the Royal Air Force Regiment, which equipped some with 20-mm. cannon in the hull front and twin Browning machine-guns in the turret).

44 **Car, 4 × 4, Light Reconnaissance, Humber, Mark IIIA and Car, 4 × 4, Light Reconnaissance, Morris, Mark II,** U.K.

The Rootes Group were responsible for the major part of the production of Light Reconnaissance cars in the United Kingdom in World War II (3,600 in total), commencing with the Mark I (known as Ironside I) of 1940. This was followed by the Mark II which had an enclosed roof mounting a small turret, and in turn by the externally similar Mark III. This model, however, introduced 4-wheel drive. It was succeeded in 1942 by the Mark IIIA, shown here, which had various minor improvements, the most noticeable of which were extra observation ports at the front corner angles of the hull. A 3½-ton vehicle powered by an 87-b.h.p. Humber six-cylinder engine, which gave it a top speed of 50 m.p.h., the armament of the Humber Mark IIIA Light Reconnaissance Car consisted normally of a 0·303-in. Bren light machine-gun mounted in the turret, to which was sometimes added a 0·55-in. Boys anti-tank rifle usually mounted in the hull front. Often a smoke discharger was also carried. The car had a crew of three, and light armour of up to 10 mm.

The Car, 4 × 2, Light Reconnaissance, Morris, Mark I was put into production by the Nuffield Group to supplement the Humbers and the later versions of the Beaverette being built by the Standard Motor Company. A rear-engined vehicle, the Morris Mark I's cross country performance was enhanced by the smooth enclosed design of its underbelly. Nevertheless, a 4-wheel drive version, the Mark II, was introduced to take the place of the Mark I. With a 71·8 b.h.p. Morris engine and weighing slightly more at 3·7 tons and with 14-mm. armour, the specification and performance of the Morris Mark II was similar to that of the Humber Mark IIIA. The layout of the armament differed, however, in that the Boys anti-tank rifle, when carried, was operated from a hatch, to the left of the turret mounting the Bren

gun, and the gunner was protected by the raised armoured hatch cover. About 2,290 Morris Marks I and II Light Reconnaissance Cars were built.

Intended originally as equipment for the Reconnaissance Corps, both the Morris and Humber Light Reconnaissance Cars were also used extensively by armoured car units of the Royal Air Force Regiment, and the Humber Mark IIIA in the illustration is one belonging to the R.A.F. Regiment in the North West Europe campaign. Both makes of car were used also for reconnoitring and liaison purposes by Royal Engineers field companies and the Morris Mark II shown is in the markings of a field company, R.E., of the 43rd (Wessex) Infantry Division.

45 Armoured Carrier, Wheeled, I.P., Mark IIA and Armoured Carrier, Wheeled, I.P., A.O.V., India.

The wheeled Armoured Carrier, Mark I, built in India in 1940–41, was followed throughout World War II by a series of armoured carriers of successive Marks—a total of 4,655 of them were built by the War's end.

A rear-engine layout was adopted for the Indian wheeled carriers after the Mark I. The Marks II, IIa and IIb were very similar to each other, the two latter having slightly larger tyres and the Mark IIb a slight modification to the roof plate. All employed chassis supplied direct from Canada by the Ford Motor Company of Canada. These were 4-wheel drive chassis with 95 b.h.p. Ford V-8 engines. The armour plate was designed and manufactured in India and assembly took place mainly at factories of the Tata Iron and Steel Co. and the East Indian Railway Workshops.

The Carrier, Wheeled, Mark IIC was very much like its predecessors in appearance but had a number of further improvements, including heavier springs and front axles, wider track, larger tyres and a 12-gallon auxiliary petrol tank. An Armoured Observation Vehicle version of the Mark IIC, with a small turret mounting a light machine-gun was built. This tended to be used as a light reconnaissance car, although there was also a Carrier, Mark III, which had a turret with a Boys 0·55-in. anti-tank rifle and a Bren 0·303-in. machine gun and was, in fact, specifically intended for this purpose.

The final version, Mark IV, differed from all earlier vehicles in that the driver sat separately from the rest of the crew in an armoured cab.

The Mark II series carriers were used in the North African campaigns, in Italy and in the South East Asia campaign, whereas the A.O.V. and the Marks III and IV are not known to have been employed outside Asia. The standard carriers, wheeled, were employed for a variety of purposes, in much the same way as the British tracked Universal-series carriers, by both infantry, artillery and reconnaissance units.

An Armoured Carrier, Wheeled, I.P., Mark IIA (with a Boys anti-tank rifle mounted, although a Bren light machine-gun was more often used), belonging to the Reconnaissance Unit (Indian Cavalry) of the 8th Indian Division in Italy in 1943 is shown, together with a Carrier, Wheeled, A.O.V. in Burma in 1945.

46 Armoured Command Vehicle (A.E.C.) 4 × 4, Mark I and Armoured Command Vehicle (A.E.C.) 6 × 6, Mark I, U.K.

The limited number of Guy Lizard and smaller Morris armoured command vehicles built at the beginning of World War II, was almost entirely replaced for the greater part of the war by vehicles on A.E.C. chassis.

The A.E.C. Matador chassis was used as the basis of the 4-wheeled A.C.V.—known at first officially as 'Lorry, 3 ton, 4 × 4, Armoured Command, A.E.C.' This consisted basically of an armoured body (12-mm. armour) fitted out internally for command purposes and carrying two wireless sets. These were a No. 19 H.P. and a No. 19 in the Low Power version, and an R.C.A. receiver and a No. 19 set in the High Power version. The A.C.V. Mark II (in a Low Power version only) differed in having an internal partition, dividing it into staff and wireless compartments.

Weighing nearly 12 tons, the A.E.C. 4 × 4 Armoured Command Vehicle was powered by an A.E.C. diesel engine of 95 b.h.p. which gave it a top speed of 35 m.p.h. No armament was fitted but a Bren light machine-gun was carried for defence.

A total of 416 4 × 4 A.C.V.s was built, and these were supplemented in 1944–45 by 151 vehicles of a new model—on an A.E.C. 6-wheel-drive chassis. This was very much more roomy than its predecessor, being 6 feet longer, but slightly lower. It was also very much heavier at 19 tons loaded, and was powered by a more powerful A.E.C. diesel engine of 135 b.h.p. Two versions were again produced, L.P. and H.P., the former having one No. 19 H.P. wireless set and one No. 19, and the latter one No. 53 and one No. 19. Both versions were divided internally, the front compartment being for staff and the rear for the wireless equipment. As in all the earlier vehicles, eight men were carried.

The A.E.C. 4 × 4 armoured command vehicles were first used in action in the North African campaign, where, incidentally, three were captured and used by German generals, two of them by Rommel himself and his staff. These two vehicles were nicknamed 'Max' and 'Moritz', although the type was given the generic name of Mammut (Mammoth) by the Germans.

The armoured command vehicles were large and conspicuous and, of course, as they carried senior officers, valuable targets, so Major Jasper Maskelyne (a well-known stage magician in civilian life) commanding a camouflage unit of the Royal Engineers, was asked to design special camouflage for them. What he did was to disguise them as ordinary lorries, similar to the standard A.E.C. Matador gun tractors which were widely used by the British Army. This involved black shadow painting on various parts of the hull, the addition of a canvas cover to the top surfaces and an extension to the armoured noseplate. This disguise is shown in the illustration of an A.E.C. 4 × 4 A.C.V. in North Africa.

47 Carrier, A.E.C., 6-pr Gun, Mark I (Deacon) and, S.P. 17-pr Gun—Straussler, U.K.

The 6-pr gun was the best British weapon available for tackling German tanks in early 1942, and the Deacon was designed as a means of increasing its mobility, chiefly for use in the North African theatre of war. The 6-pr (on a field-type, not a tank mounting) was mounted on a turntable, with a light shield open only at the rear, and carried on an armoured A.E.C. Matador chassis. The Deacon weighed 12 tons and powered by an A.E.C. six-cylinder 95-b.h.p. diesel engine had a top speed of only 19 m.p.h. Despite their bulk and slowness, the Deacons did good work in the North African campaign, after which they were handed over to the Turkish Government. A total of 150 was built in 1942 and they were supplied ex-works already painted in a bright sand yellow. A further twenty-five vehicles without the gun and a platform body were built as armoured ammunition carriers.

In 1943, an experimental wheeled self-propelled mounting for the new and very much more powerful 17-pr anti-tank gun was designed by Nicholas Straussler. Entirely original in concept, the 17-pr gun with split trail was, in effect, added to a rectangular skeleton chassis. A motive unit, consisting of Bedford type QL lorry components, was added, the engine (at the right-hand side of the chassis) driving the two front wheels for transport. When the gun was in position, the two rear wheels could be swivelled until they were at right angles to the front wheels. The right hand rear wheel could then be driven through a power take-off from the engine, so enabling the whole carriage to be rotated through 360 degrees. Sometimes known as Monitor, the Straussler S.P. 17-pr was not adopted for service because it was felt that the mounting offered insufficient protection for the gun and its crew. The illustration shows the vehicle in its travelling position.

48 Ford Armoured Cars (Arab Legion), Transjordan.

The Arab Legion of Transjordan (now the Kingdom of Jordan) originally had the tasks of patrolling the frontier and of internal security but after the outbreak of war the Arab Legion, now including a mobile unit known as the Desert Mechanized Force, served alongside the British Army in the Middle East, and was in action in Iraq and Syria in 1941. Following the success of the Arab Legion in these operations, it was decided to expand the Desert Mechanized Force, which included only six armoured cars, into a mechanized regiment (and subsequently into a mechanized brigade of three regiments).

The original six armoured cars of the Arab Legion were purchased in Palestine and were very similar to some used by the Palestine Police. No further supplies from this source, or from Britain, were available to equip the new mechanized regiments, and it was decided that the Arab Legion should build its own armoured cars in Transjordan. Four hundred Ford commercial truck chassis were ordered from the United States, although only 250 were delivered, the ships carrying the balance being torpedoed *en route*.

The Arab Legion armoured cars were designed by their commander, Glubb Pasha (John B. Glubb), and were modelled broadly on the original six vehicles (the first type of Arab Legion armoured car), which also used Ford chassis. Glubb's original model (called here for convenience the Arab Legion 2nd type) had built-up front mudguards and bevelled edges on the bonnet and front corners of the hull, but his second model (Arab Legion 3rd type) used the original truck mudguards and had a simpler bonnet design. In both models, the turret had provision for a mounted machine-gun (usually a Vickers 0·303-in.) and a Boys 0·55-in. anti-tank rifle, and an anti-aircraft machine-gun (often a Lewis 0·303-in.). Some cars were fitted with wireless, carried in the hull behind the turret. As supplies of armour plate were not available, the armour was made up of a double skin of mild steel with a sheet of plywood sandwiched between the plates.

A total of 100 armoured cars of these two types was built, and they equipped the Arab Legion mechanized regiments until being replaced by Marmon-Herrington Mark IV F armoured cars in 1945.

49 Autocanon Dodge and Autocanon 75-mm., Ford, France.

The Fighting French contingent which fought alongside British forces in the North African campaign in 1942–43, included an armoured car unit which was equipped partly with South African built Marmon-Herrington armoured cars and partly with vehicles of French design, although based on

American or Canadian chassis. This unit was formed from what was originally an infantry regiment of soldiers from French Morocco—the 1er Regiment de marche de Spahis Marocains (R.M.S.M.).

The Marmon-Herrington armoured cars (Mark III) supplied to the Fighting French were armed with machine-guns only, but these were supported by a number of vehicles (captured from the Vichy French in Syria) that were equipped with a French short 37-mm. gun and a 7·5-mm. machine-gun coaxially mounted in a small turret, open at the rear. A further 7·5-mm. machine-gun could be mounted on a pillar mount in the body of the vehicle. The chassis used for these armoured cars was a 4 × 2 U.S.-built Dodge 1940 model. The lorry cab was retained (with the addition of light windscreen armour) and only the rear part was fully armoured, although, even so, the back portion had an open top.

Later in 1943, the R.M.S.M. received a number of vehicles with very much greater fire power, designed by one of their officers, Lieutenant Conus. This type was based on the Ford F 60L 3-ton lorry supplied by Canada for the British Army. A French 75-mm. field gun was mounted at the rear (using the turntable from a captured Italian tank) where it had a full 360 degrees traverse. The crew were protected by a three-sided shield, and the rear of the chassis and the driver's cab were also armoured, although the latter appears to have been mainly to protect the driver from the blast of the gun. An anti-aircraft pillar mounting for a machine-gun was provided on the front of the gun shield. A lorry canvas hood

was carried to disguise the gun when not in action. These 'autocanons' were used in action from about October 1942 until the end of the North African campaign.

These two types of Fighting French equipment are shown in the illustrations in typical Middle East colours, the Dodge bearing a French registration number and the Ford F 60L still carrying its original British W.D. number.

50 Carro Armato M.15/42, Italy.

The Italian medium tank M.15/42 was a logical development of the M.13/40 of 1940 and its derivative the M.14/41. Very much like its predecessors in appearance, the M.15/42's 47-mm. gun was, however, of 40 calibres length (compared with 32 calibres of the earlier tanks) which gave it a far higher muzzle velocity and greater penetrative power.

The other most important change compared with the M.13/40 and M.14/41 was a more powerful engine, the S.P.A. 15TB which produced 192 b.h.p. and gave a better maximum (road) speed of 25 m.p.h., despite the increase of a ton in weight. Although the new engine provided the extra power needed, it was a petrol engine and it seems to have been something of a backward step to abandon the diesel type previously used.

Other features of the M.15/42 were a crew of four, an armament of three 8-mm. Breda machine-guns (one coaxial, two in a dual mount in the front of the hull) besides the 47-mm. gun; and maximum armour protection of 45-mm. (50-mm. on the gun mantlet).

About 2,000 M.13/40s and M.14/41s were completed (of which about the last 800 were the latter) but production of the Carro Armato M.15/42 ceased after only 82 of them were built by early 1943. Following this, Italian armoured fighting vehicle production was concentrated on self-propelled guns.

One illustration shows the fifth tank of the 1st Company, 2nd Platoon, of an Italian armoured battalion in Italy in 1943; the other an M.15/42 in desert colours.

51 Carro Armato P.40, Italy.

The only Italian heavy tank of World War II, the P.40, which entered production in 1943, had its origin in design studies commenced in 1938. One of two Ansaldo designs (in competition with two drawn up by the official Direzione della Motorizzazione) was chosen in 1940, although the first prototype to be built did not appear until early 1942.

A 26-ton vehicle, protected up to a maximum of 50 mm., a high velocity 75-mm. gun was chosen as the main armament. As the gun being developed for it was not ready when the prototype was completed, however, the 75/18 howitzer was mounted instead. This was replaced in the second prototype by the interim gun 75/32 until, with the third prototype, the 75/34, with a muzzle velocity of 610 metres per second, could be used.

The suspension of the P.40 followed the common Italian practice of two groups of four road wheels each side carried on a semi-elliptic leaf spring for each group—a somewhat crude but well-tried system. The hull and turret layout were conventional, the armament of the 75-mm. gun and coaxial 8-mm. machine-gun being concentrated in the turret—the front hull machine-gun which existed in the first two prototypes was eliminated in the final version.

The engine was at the rear, the transmission being led forward via the gearbox and clutch to track drive sprockets at the front. The prototypes used a 330-h.p. diesel but a new twelve-cylinder-V petrol engine of 420 h.p. was ready for use in the production models, to which it gave a maximum speed of 25 m.p.h.

Only twenty-one P.40s had been completed by the time of the Armistice in 1943. Two Italian tank battalions to be equipped with P.40s were in the process of formation at this time, but in the end only the Germans employed in service the few P.40s available.

52 Semovente M. 42M da 75/34 and Semovente M.42L da 105/23, Italy.

Some of the most effective Italian armoured fighting vehicles were the series of assault guns based on medium tank chassis which appeared from 1941 onwards.

These vehicles were fully armoured and enclosed, and mounted weapons ranging in power from the 75/18 (75-mm.; 18 calibres long) howitzer originally used on the M.13/40 chassis, to the 105/23 on the M.15/42 chassis.

The 75/18 Semovente was in production between 1941 and 1943: later vehicles used the M.14/41 and M.15/42 chassis. In all, 780 vehicles were built. They gave good service with the Ariete and Littorio Divisions in North Africa and later on Italian soil.

A new weapon for the P.40 tank and assault guns, the 75/34, was in the process of development in 1942. In the meantime as an interim measure the 75/32 was introduced, although only a few dozen assault guns of this type were built, by the Ansaldo concern.

The prototype for the Semovente 75/34 was completed by the end of 1942, by which time a total of 500 had been ordered. Due to problems over the design of the mounting for the 75/34, however, 75/18s or 75/32s were fitted in M.15/42 chassis intended for the new gun. In the end, only just over ninety 75/34 assault guns were built. They were intended to replace the artillery in the armoured units, the 75/18s then to be transferred to support the infantry of armoured formations. Their main use was, however, by the Germans, who acquired all those available in Italy in 1943.

The Semovente M.42M da 75/34 was considered to be a good 'tank hunter', its gun having a muzzle velocity of 610 metres per second and a range of 12¼ kilometres. Apart from the longer gun, it was similar in most external respects to the early 75/18 and 75/32 assault guns on the chassis of M.13/40, M.14/41 and M.15/42 tanks, all of which had similar running gear. Weighing 15 tons, the Semovente M.42M da 75/34 was powered by a S.P.A. eight-cylinder petrol engine of 192 b.h.p. which gave it a top speed of about 25 m.p.h. The vehicle had a crew of three men and an 8-mm. machine-gun was carried for anti-aircraft defence.

The Semovente M.42L da 105/23 was in general appearance like the 75-mm. assault gun but had a much larger 105-mm., 23-calibre length, howitzer, specially developed as an assault gun. The final prototype was ready in January 1943, and firing trials took place later in that month. Deliveries began in May 1943 but, although 454 of them were finally ordered, only a relatively small number was completed. Part of the artillery group of the Ariete Division was equipped with Semovente 105/23s in the summer of 1943. Some of these assault guns were used by Italian units in the defence of Rome in September 1943. Later the Germans requisitioned all those available and employed them in Italy.

With the same 192-b.h.p. petrol engine, the Semovente 105/23 weighed somewhat more at 15·6 tons than earlier models and had a top speed of 22 m.p.h. The 105-mm. gun was a good anti-tank weapon, notably with the special ammunition developed for it and, mounted in a compact chassis, this combination represented one of the best Italian armoured fighting vehicles of World War II.

53 **Panzerkampfwagen II, Ausf.L, Luchs,** Germany.

The PzKpfw II as a battle tank was, as early as 1940, recognized as being outdated. Its development, as a reconnaissance vehicle was, however, continued and the final model, Ausf.L, known as Luchs (Lynx) was produced in 1942–43.

Although retaining the same general layout of the earlier vehicles of the

PzKpfw II series, the Ausf.L's design was derived mainly from Daimler-Benz prototypes (based on their earlier Ausf.D and E) rather than the M.A.N. design used for the great majority of PzKfw IIs built. The main external difference of the Ausf.L from all earlier production PzKpfw IIs was the overlapping road wheels, with torsion bar suspension, and wide tracks. With a maximum armour thickness of 30-mm. (excluding spaced armour added later to some vehicles), the armament of the Luchs consisted of a 2-cm. gun and one machine-gun, mounted coaxially in the turret. A few vehicles were fitted instead with a 5-cm. gun—a fairly heavy weapon for a vehicle of under 12 tons. The engine of the Luchs was a 178-b.h.p. six-cylinder Maybach which gave it a maximum speed of about 40 m.p.h.

54 Panzerkampfwagen III, Ausf.L and Ausf.M, Germany.

Production of the PzKpfw III, the first models of which were built in 1937, was not finally ceased until the summer of 1943, when it was still an important element in the German armoured forces. Successive increases in armament, from the 3·7-cm. gun of the early models, through the 5-cm. L/42 of 1940 to the long 5-cm. L/60 of the late models, Ausf.L and M, associated with increased armour protection, justified the retention of the PzKpfw III. Even when superseded as a tank, the Panzer III chassis remained in production as the basis of assault guns.

Among the features shared by the Ausf.L and M with earlier models of the PzKpfw III were the transverse torsion-bar suspension system and the twelve-cylinder Maybach engine of 300-h.p. and the secondary armament of one machine-gun coaxial with the gun in the turret and one machine-gun in the right side of the hull, beside the driver. The maximum armour protection of the Ausf.L and M was 70-mm. in spaced armour at the front and the combination of the increased armour and heavier gun made it necessary to reinforce the suspension. Skirt armour on hull sides and turret was also carried on some tanks. The Ausf.L and M were almost identical in appearance but in the latter, to simplify production, some vision ports and the hull escape doors were eliminated—with the introduction of skirt armour, these were, in any case, of little use.

The final version of PzKpfw III, the Ausf.N was the same as Ausf.L or M but with the short-barrelled 7·5-cm. KwK L/24. In all, 5,644 PzKpfw IIIs were produced between 1937 and 1943.

The upper illustration shows a PzKpfw III, Ausf.M, and the lower one a PzKpfw III, Ausf.L, in winter camouflage in Russia, with the guns sheathed as protection from the cold.

55 Panzerkampfwagen IV, Ausf.H, Germany.

The Panzerkampfwagen IV, which originally entered production on a limited scale in 1937, was steadily improved in armament and armour during World War II so that it remained in production right to the end of the war, by which time about 9,000 of them had been completed. The fact that, latterly, production was continued mainly because of the urgent need for serviceable tanks in large numbers, rather than changing completely to a more modern design, is no reflection on the excellent basic design of the PzKpfw IV.

A medium tank originally specified in the 20-ton class, although in its final form at around 25 tons, the Panzer IV was powered by a 300-b.h.p. twelve-cylinder Maybach at the rear with the gearbox and final drive sprockets at the front. The suspension consisted of eight road wheels each side, suspended in pairs on leaf springs.

When the Ausf.H appeared in 1943, the main armament was the long-barrelled 7·5-cm. L/48, increasingly powerful guns having been introduced in successive models, starting with the low-velocity 7·5-cm. L/24 of the early Panzer IVs. The secondary armament remained as two machine-guns—one in the hull front and one in the turret, coaxial with the 7·5-cm. gun. The maximum armour protection was 80-mm., having been increased four-fold over that of the original version, Ausf.A. Skirting plates (or wire mesh, in some cases) were often added to the turret and hull sides to give protection against hollow charge projectiles.

The Ausf.J, which followed, the final version of PzKpfw IV, was very similar externally to the preceding model but incorporated detail changes. One of the most important (and a retrograde step) was the deletion of the turret power traverse, leaving only a 2-speed hand traverse system, in order to make room for increased fuel capacity (680 litres, compared with 470 for Ausf H) to give the extra range called for by 1944.

One of the illustrations shows a tank partly painted with 'Zimmerit', an anti-magnetic paste to repel sticky bombs; both tanks shown have both hull and turret skirting plates.

56 Panzerkampfwagen V, Panther, Germany.

The Panther, together with the Russian T-34 which was the direct cause of its inception, was one of the best tanks of World War II and one which has had much influence on post-war tank design.

Once the full effect of the T-34 was appreciated, it was at first proposed that a close copy should be built in Germany to counter it, but this was soon proved to be impracticable because of the fresh tooling that would have been required and the absence of suitable raw materials. The main features of the T.34 were, however, reproduced in the two designs submitted, ranging from the Daimler-Benz VK 3002, which was closely similar to the T.34, to the M.A.N. version, which had more traditional German features. In spite of Hitler's preference for the Daimler-Benz design, the M.A.N. model was chosen for production, which commenced in November 1942.

The Panther, as the Pzkpfw V was named, had the long sloping glacis plate of the T.34, inward sloping hull sides above track level, a turret mounting a long 7·5-cm. gun (L/70—70 calibres long) and interleaved road wheels, sprung on transverse torsion bars. Armour protection was at a maximum of 120-mm. on the turret and 80-mm. on the hull. A Maybach twelve-cylinder engine developing 642-b.h.p. (increased to 690-b.h.p. in the later models, Ausf.A and G) gave a top speed of about 28 m.p.h.

The Ausf.D was followed in production by the illogically designated Ausf.A which incorporated various improvements, one of the most obvious of which was the replacement of the unusual vertical-letter box type of mounting for the hull machine-gun by a more conventional ball-mounting. The turret was equipped with a new type of cupola and the pistol ports and loading door, present in the Ausf.D, were eliminated.

The final model of Panther, Ausf.G, had further changes, partly to compensate for shortages of raw materials and to simplify production. The driver's vision port was replaced by a rotating periscope, leaving the glacis plate clear except for the machine-gun ball mount; the hull sides were more sloped and stowage boxes at the rear were included inside the armour. This latter change was not always apparent, however, as side skirting plates were always likely to be fitted on all models of Panther. Finally, later production vehicles had all-steel road wheels with resilient hubs instead of the rubber-tyred wheels used earlier.

The illustrations show a Panther Ausf.D (bottom view) and an Ausf.G.

57 **Panzerkampfwagen VI, Tiger I,** Germany.

Perhaps the tank which created the greatest impression on British troops in World War II, from the time it was first encountered by them in Tunisia in 1943, was the Tiger. First used in action in September 1942 in Russia, the Tiger's design was completed before features exemplified by the Russian T.34 could be incorporated. Nevertheless, the heavy armour (at a maximum of 110-mm. on the turret and 100-mm. on the hull) and the powerful 8·8-cm. gun (KwK 36 L/55) made the Tiger a very formidable tank right to the end of the war.

Work on various heavy tank projects was started as early as 1937. These were modified with changing requirements and with the incorporation of an 8·8-cm. gun resulted in 1942 in the specification V.K. 4501, for which the design competition was won by the Henschel firm.

In spite of its size, the Tiger was fairly conventional in layout and design except that interleaved road wheels in the suspension system were used for the first time in a production tank although they were, of course, already a familiar feature in German half-tracks.

The engine—at the rear, the transmission being led forward via an 8-speed gearbox to front drive sprockets—was a V-form twelve-cylinder Maybach of 650-b.h.p., increased to 700-b.h.p. in the later vehicles to be built. This produced a top speed of 24 m.p.h., quite satisfactory for a 54-ton tank.

A total of 1,350 Tiger Is was manufactured and they were used in action in North Africa, Sicily, Italy, North West Europe and Russia.

58 **Panzerkampfwagen VI, Tiger II,** Germany.

Known to the Western Allies as King Tiger or Royal Tiger, the Tiger II or

Tiger Ausf. B was even more feared by its opponents than Tiger I. With an even more powerful gun (8·8-cm., 71 calibres long, compared with Tiger I's 56 calibres) thicker armour and a sloping hull glacis plate, the Tiger II had all the best features of its predecessor, together with improvements suggested by experience in Russia. Development of the type was called for in the autumn of 1942 and when the Tiger IIs were delivered to the troops in 1944 they were the most powerful tanks in service in the world, as well as the heaviest, and the position remained unchanged until nearly the end of the War.

Fortunately for its opponents, the Tiger II was mechanically unreliable, a fault perhaps due to insufficient time being allowed for development. Fourteen tons heavier than Tiger I, the King Tiger had a similar mechanical layout but the road wheels, sprung on independent torsion bars, were not interleaved, as in Tiger I, although they were overlapped. Four hundred and eighty-five Tiger IIs were built, of which the first fifty had different, more rounded, turrets than had been built for a Porsche-designed Tiger II, although the Porsche tank itself was rejected.

The relatively few Tiger IIs built were used in 1944–45 with considerable effect on both Germany's East and West fronts.

59 **Panzerkampfwagen Maus and Panzerkampfwagen E.100,** Germany.

These two colossal tanks, Maus and E.100, weighing around 150 tons, were produced in prototype form in Germany in 1944–45.

Maus, the earlier of the two, was the result of an instruction by Hitler to Dr Porsche in 1942 to design in conjunction with Krupp's a super-heavy tank in the 100-ton class. The first prototype (without turret and armament) was running by December 1944. The turret, mounted at the rear, with an armament consisting of a 15-cm. L/38 gun with a coaxial 7·5-m. KwK was only fitted at a late stage in development of the prototype, most test runs being carried out with a simulated turret.

The final all-up weight of Maus was no less than 185 tons, which few bridges could have withstood, so provision was made for the tank to ford rivers up to a depth of 14 feet, with air supply through a submarine-type snorkel tube. A 1200-b.h.p. Daimler-Benz petrol engine (a diesel was the ultimate type) with electric transmission was used and this produced a top speed of 12 m.p.h.

Panzerkampfwagen E.100 was the 'official' design by the Army Weapons Department for a tank in the 100-ton class and the heaviest in a proposed family of tracked fighting vehicles of between 5 and 100 tons, in which it was hoped to standardize as many components as possible. A somewhat more conventional design than Maus, being developed by Adler from the basis of the Tiger series, the E.100 was rather like a scaled-up Tiger II in appearance, with a 15-cm. gun and a coaxial 7·5-cm. gun in the turret, which was mounted centrally. The engine was a 700-b.h.p. twelve-cylinder Maybach for trials, although a 1,200-b.h.p.

version was proposed and was needed to produce the required performance.

The suspension system, like that of Maus, abandoned the torsion bars used for the later German medium and heavy tanks. It used a form of coil springing—Belleville washers. The weight of E.100 was about 138 tons and the maximum armour protection for both Maus and E.100 was 240-mm.

Two prototypes of the Maus were completed and tested in 1944–45; the E.100 prototype was never finished. Although overcoming engineering problems in the design of such heavy vehicles, the tactical value of tanks of this size was questionable as was, to an even greater degree, the diversion of A.F.V. design and production effort. There was certainly little excuse at all for two separate and competing designs at a critical stage of the war for Germany.

60 **Jagdpanzer 38(t), Hetzer,** Germany.

The Jagdpanzer 38(t) Hetzer ('Baiter') was one of the best self-propelled mountings for its size of World War II, being compact, well-armoured and mobile, with a top speed of about 25 m.p.h. The gun—the 7·5-cm. Pak 39 (L/48) was mounted in the right-hand side of the sloping glacis plate, which was armoured to a maximum of 60-mm. The driver sat at the left, the 150-b.h.p. six-cylinder Praga engine being at the rear. The suspension was of the leaf spring variety, the large road wheels being sprung in pairs.

An interesting feature of the Jagdpanzer 38(t) was the type of machine-gun mounted on the roof in some vehicles. This was fitted with a deflection device which enabled it to 'fire round corners', thus making it more effective in close-up defence.

The last type on the Czech LT-38 chassis to go into production, 1,577 Hetzers were built in 1944 and the design was considered good enough to be adopted by the Swiss Army in the post-war years.

61 **Sturmgeheschütz III/10·5-cm. StuH,** Germany.

The Sturmgeschütz III was one of Germany's most enduring armoured fighting vehicles, production of which commenced in 1940 and continued right through to the end of the war, when over 10,500 vehicles had been built.

In its standard form the StuG III was originally equipped with the low-velocity 7·5-cm. L/24 gun, suitable for close support of infantry. This was replaced in 1942 by the much more powerful L/43 and L/48 weapons which were also capable of tackling tanks. Also developed in 1943 was a new version for the close support role, but with a much heavier gun—the 10·5-cm. howitzer. The first vehicles had the 1eFH18 (light field howitzer) but the StuH.42 (assault howitzer) was soon standardized for the majority of 10·5-cm. StuG. III that were produced.

The chassis of the StuG III remained throughout production that of the contemporary model of Pzkpfw III, although the tank itself was eventually withdrawn from production in favour of the assault gun. The armour protection in the later StuG III was at a maximum of 80-mm. and side skirting plates were usually fitted. The total weight was nearly 24 tons, although the maximum speed of 24 m.p.h. remained the same as in earlier models.

The upper illustration shows a vehicle with 'Zimmerit' finish and skirting plates.

62 Sturmpanzer IV, Brummbär and Jagdpanzer IV/70, Germany.

Two self-propelled mountings developed from the Stu.G III concept, but taking advantage of the greater scope offered by the larger Pz IV chassis, the Brummbär (Grizzly Bear) appeared in 1943 and the Jagdpanzer IV/70 in 1944.

Armed with the short (12 calibres) heavy 15-cm. StuH.43, the Brummbär was armoured to a maximum of 100-mm. on the front plate. Weighing over 28 tons the chassis was overloaded, although a top speed of 25 m.p.h. was attainable. Only 315 of them were built and to compensate for a shortcoming discovered in service, the last ones produced had a machine-gun added in a ball-mounting at the left-hand side of the sloping front plate.

The Jagdpanzer IV/70 was the outcome of the policy to produce heavily armoured turretless self-propelled anti-tank guns at the expense of tank production—a token of the realization of Germany's need for vehicles suited more for defence than attack. In addition, production of turretless vehicles rather than tanks helped to increase the total number available. Earlier vehicles on the PzKpfw IV chassis used the 7·5-cm. L/48 in a superstructure like that of the Stu.G III until the redesigned Jagdpanzer IV appeared. At first also

armed with the 7·5-cm. L/48, the final version had the powerful 7·5-cm. L/70—the same gun as the Panther's. This exceptionally long weapon caused nose heaviness, resulting in heavy wear on the rubber tyres of the front two road wheels each side. Accordingly, steel-tyred resilient road wheels were substituted in these positions. Also, to simplify the suspension, only three, instead of four, return rollers each side were used in the later vehicles built. Output of Jagdpanzer IV with both the L/48 and L/70 guns (mostly the former) amounted to over 1,500 vehicles.

63 8.8-cm. Panzerjäger Panther-Jagdpanther, Germany.

Like the tank on which it was based, the Jagdpanther was a formidable vehicle. Following the standard German practice of using a tank chassis to mount a heavier gun in a limited traverse mounting, thus keeping the weight within reasonable bounds, the Panther chassis was used to create a highly mobile heavily armed 'tank hunter'.

The running gear and lower chassis of the Panther (Ausf.G) was retained but the hull was increased in height and the gun—the 8·8-cm. L/71 (71 calibres long)—was mounted in the centre of the sloping glacis plate. A ball-mounted machine-gun was retained but higher up the glacis than in the tank.

Produced in 1944 the Jagdpanther was considered by some at the time to be an undesirable dilution of Panther production, but in the defensive operations of 1944-45, the Jagdpanther was probably an even more effective weapon than the tank.

64 Jagdpanzer Tiger (P), Elefant, Germany.

Dr Ferdinand Porsche's design to the V.K. 4501 specification—the Tiger tank—had interesting and unusual features, such as petrol-electric drive and longitudinal torsion-bar suspension, but the more conventional Henschel design was chosen for the production order for the Tiger. Nevertheless, a limited order for ninety Porsche Tiger chassis was awarded. Five were completed at the Nibelungenwerke in Austria as tanks (and used for trials only) and the rest were modified at the Alkett concern in Berlin as 'tank hunters'. This involved the addition of a fixed superstructure (armoured to a maximum of 200-mm.) in which an 8·8-cm. Pak L/71 was mounted, with a limited traverse. The original engine intended by Porsche was replaced by two twelve-cylinder Maybach engines, totalling 640-b.h.p. but the electric transmission was retained. Weighing 67 tons, the top speed was only $12\frac{1}{2}$ m.p.h.

Named at first Ferdinand (after Dr Porsche) and later Elefant, these Jagdpanzers were employed at first in Russia and later, in reduced numbers, in Italy. Experience in Russia showed that the lack of a hull machine-gun was a serious fault, and one was incorporated later.

65 Jagdpanzer VI—Jagdtiger, Germany.

In accordance with the usual German practice, a companion 'tank hunter' version of Tiger II was produced, in which the rotating turret was replaced by a fixed superstructure mounting a heavier gun than that carried in the tank. This was the Jagdtiger, armed with a 12·8-cm. Pak 44 L/55—the most powerfully armed fighting vehicle to go into production in World War II, although Germany's circumstances in 1944 made it possible for a total of only forty-eight to be built. With a similar power train and suspension (although lengthened) to that of Tiger II, the Jagdtiger was protected to a maximum thickness of no less than 250-mm., weighed 70 tons and had a top speed of 23 m.p.h. It was the heaviest and one of the most formidable fighting vehicles of its era to enter service.

During the course of its short production life, the suspension of the Jagdtiger was changed from the Henschel system of transverse torsion bars used in Tiger II to a longitudinal torsion bar system, designed by Ferdinand Porsche, in which the wheels were mounted in four pairs each side. In the illustrations a vehicle with the Porsche suspension is shown at the top, and a Jagdtiger with the Henschel system, which had nine overlapped wheels each side instead of eight, at the bottom.

66 7·5-cm. Pak auf Gw. 38(t), Marder III, Ausf.M, Germany.

The Czech LT-38 tank was continued in production after the German takeover of Czechoslovakia. By 1942, the Pzkpfw 38(t), as it was then called, was outclassed as a battle tank, but it was thought well worth while to continue output of the reliable, sturdy and easily maintained chassis as a mounting for self-propelled weapons.

The earlier self-propelled mountings (Geschützwagen—Gw.) used the chassis with the original layout in which the engine was located at the rear. The later versions, built in 1943–44, had the engine (a six-cylinder 150-b.h.p. Praga) moved forward to a position alongside the driver, and were designated Ausf.M (M = mitte [middle]), the earlier version being Ausf.H = heckmotor [rear engine]). Apart from better weight distribution, a lower silhouette was possible with the engine relocated and there were advantages in the crew having access to the gun from the rear.

The weapon used was the 7·5-cm. Pak 40/3, of a calibre length of 46, and mounted behind a shield open at the rear and with no overhead protection. One machine-gun was usually carried for local defence.

Seven hundred and ninety-nine Marder III, Ausf.M were built in 1943–44, together with four hundred and eighteen of the earlier Ausf.H in 1942–43.

Two views of different vehicles are shown in the illustrations.

67   15-cm. sIG33 auf Sf. II and 7·62-cm. Pak auf Gw. II, Ausf. D, Germany.

These two self-propelled mountings both used the chassis of different models of the PzKpfw II. The heavy infantry gun (sIG) carrier was, however, by far the better vehicle, being low and inconspicuous and the addition of an extra road wheel each side in the later version (which appeared in 1943) gave a better weight distribution and more space for crew and ammunition. With

a crew of five and a loaded weight of about 13 tons this self-propelled gun (Selbstfahrlafettc—Sfl.), which was powered by the standard six-cylinder 140-b.h.p. Maybach engine, had a top speed of 25 m.p.h. Vehicles of this type on both lengthened and normal PzII chassis were used in North Africa and Russia.

The 7·62-cm. Pak—a captured Russian anti-tank gun, rechambered to take German ammunition—on the Pzkpfw II Ausf. D (also Ausf. E) chassis was, by contrast, one of the crudest of the improvised self-propelled mountings produced by the Germans in World War II. Nevertheless, it served its purpose in helping to get the greatest possible number of anti-tank guns into the field in the shortest possible time. The long-barrelled gun, protected by its own shield, was mounted towards the rear of the vehicle on top of the armoured superstructure with the end of the barrel projecting over the front. The Ausf.D of Pzkpfw II had a 180-b.h.p. six-cylinder Maybach engine and the Gw II for the 7·62-cm. Pak weighing 11·5 tons had a top speed of about 35 m.p.h.

68   15-cm. Pz. fH 18 auf Gw. III/IV, Hummel and 8.8-cm. Pak43/ I (L/71) auf Gw. III/IV, Nashorn, Germany.

A modified Panzer IV chassis, incorporating features of the Panzer III, was used between 1942 and 1944 for the production of two specially designed heavily armed but relatively lightly armoured self-propelled mountings. Known as Geschützwagen III/IV, the chassis had the Panzer IV suspension with the engine (300-b.h.p. twelve-cylinder Maybach) moved forward to allow room for a fighting compartment at the rear.

Hummel (Bumble Bee) was the 15-cm. field Howitzer (Pz.H.18) on this chassis: 666 vehicles were built in 1943–44, together with 150 similar vehicles without guns for use as armoured ammunition carriers.

The 8·8-cm. Pak 43/1 (L/71) on the same chassis with minor variations for the gun mounting, ammunition stowage etc. was known at first as Hornisse (Hornet) and later as Nashorn (Rhinoceros). Four hundred and seventy three were made in 1943–44 and although, like Hummel, armoured only to a maximum of 30-mm., the powerful gun made them a formidable weapon.

69 Flakpanzer IV (3·7-cm.), Möbelwagen and Flakpanzer IV (2-cm.), Wirbelwind, Germany.

The overwhelming Allied air superiority by 1943 made it increasingly necessary for Germany to direct a greater proportion of armoured fighting vehicle production to the output of anti-aircraft tanks.

The Pzkpfw IV chassis was used for some of the more important of the A.A. tank designs which entered service in 1943–44. The commonest of the lighter weapons were the quadruple 20-mm. and the single 3·7-cm. guns. The earlier design for both of these mountings (called Möbelwagen—furniture van—in the case of the 3·7-cm. mounting) consisted of the guns with their normal shield, surrounded by a hinged four-

sided square armoured structure, which folded flat, when required, to give unimpeded all-round traverse.

The later design, again generally similar for both 20-mm. and 3·7-cm. guns called Wirbelwind (Whirlwind) for the former and Ostwind (East Wind) for the latter, dispensed with the clumsy folding shields and used instead a multi-sided pot-shaped turret, open at the top. Although only lightly armoured (16-mm.) this turret gave better protection to the gun crew.

In addition to the anti-aircraft weapon, Wirbelwind and Ostwind (unlike the Möbelwagen types) retained the front hull machine-gun of the standard Pzkpfw IV.

70 Schwerer Ladungsträger (Sdkfz 301) and Leichter Ladungsträger (SdKfz 302), Germany.

These two machines, heavy and light demolition vehicles, were more commonly known as B.IV and Goliath, respectively. The B.IV, designed by the Borgward company of Bremen and produced from 1942 onwards, carried a 500 kg. explosive charge in a wedge-shaped bin at the front. With a seat for one man, the B.IV could be driven close to the scene of the action. In the attack, the vehicle was radio controlled. At the target, the bolts holding the demolition charge were destroyed by an electrically detonated charge, allowing the explosive bin to slide to the ground. The vehicle was then reversed away before the demolition charge was detonated. Powered by a petrol engine, the B.IV could be controlled by radio up to distances of about 1¼ miles. The first model, Ausf. A, shown in the illustration, weighed 3·6 tons. A total of 1,193 B.IVs (in three models) was produced between 1942 and 1944. They were used chiefly by heavy tank units to help destroy fixed defences.

The lighter demolition vehicle SdKfz 302 or 'Goliath' was, unlike the B.IV, expendable. About 5 ft 4 in. long, the Goliath (Ausf. A) carried a 60 kg. explosive charge. Driven by one electrical starter motor for each track, the vehicle was guided, and detonated when it reached its target, through a 3-core electric cable, of which about 670 yards was carried on a drum at the rear. In front of the drum was a compartment containing the control gear and the explosive was in a third compartment. Some 2,650 Goliaths of this type were built between 1942 and 1944 together with 5,079 (between 1943 and 1945) of a later and slightly heavier model, Ausf. B or SdKfz 303, powered by a Zündapp petrol engine. The employment of Goliaths was similar to that of the B.IV.

In the illustration of a Goliath (Ausf.A) the cover over the rear compartment is shown raised, revealing the electric control cable reel.

71 Leichter Schützenpanzerwagen SdKfz 250/8 and Leichter Schützenpanzerwagen SdKfz 250/9, Germany

The light armoured semi-tracked armoured personnel carrier SdKfz 250 which first appeared in action as a troop carrier in 1940, had by the end of the war appeared in twelve main variants, many of which were support vehicles for the basic infantry carrier.

The SdKfz 250/8 was a self-propelled mounting for the 7·5-cm. KwK L/24—the gun used in the earliest versions of the Sturmgeschütz III although in a 6-ton vehicle only light protection could be afforded. The gun was mounted just behind the driver together with a machine-gun (MG 42) both for ranging the 7·5-cm. KwK and for general targets.

Virtually a semi-tracked light armoured car (Panzerspähwagen) the SdKfz 250/9 had the same turret as the Leichter Panzerspähwagen SdKfz 222. This turret carried a 2-cm. gun and machine-gun on a mounting also capable of anti-aircraft fire: the only overhead protection was a hinged wire mesh frame to guard against grenades.

With good mobility and a high top speed of nearly 40 m.p.h., the SdKfz 250 series were powered by a Maybach six-cylinder engine of 100-b.h.p., which drove the tracks via front drive sprockets. The front wheels were for steering only and were not driven. An efficient vehicle, although with a somewhat complicated suspension and track design making heavy demands on maintenance time, the SdKfz 250 and its larger counterpart the SdKfz 251 was not replaced in production by semi-tracks of simpler design until 1944.

72 Panzerspähwagen SdKfz 234/2 (Puma) and Panzerspähwagen SdKfz 234/3, Germany.

An improved version of the successful German eight-wheeled armoured car, first issued in 1938, appeared in 1944. Although the chassis was basically unaltered and only minor changes were made to the armoured hull, the use of a diesel engine of greatly increased power (the Czechoslovakian Tatra twelve-cylinder V-form of 220-b.h.p.) led to improved performance. An air-cooled diesel engine was specified in 1940, when the design work began, with the object of facilitating operation in hot countries but this type of engine was also an advantage in subsequent operations in the cold weather in Russia and the fuel economy of the diesel resulted in a much wider range.

The first model of the new eight-wheeled armoured car, SdKfz 234/1, was armed only with a 2-cm. KwK and one machine-gun in an open-topped turret—no more than that of the 5-ton light armoured car SdKfz 222, and very inadequate for a vehicle of this size. The next model, SdKfz 234/2, was equipped with a 5-cm. (L/60) gun and a machine-gun in an enclosed turret, which made it capable of engaging tanks, although it was still intended only as a reconnaissance vehicle.

Two further models of the SdKfz 234 were produced as self-propelled mountings with guns mounted to fire forwards, with only limited traverse. The SdKfz 234/4 was a highly mobile 'tank hunter' with a 7·5-cm. Pak L/48 and the SdKfz 234/3—shown in one of the illustrations, together with SdKfz 234/2—was a close support vehicle with the low velocity 7·5-cm. Stu.K L/24.

73 T-34 ('T-34/76B') and T-34/85 (Medium Tanks), U.S.S.R.

The immense superiority of the T-34 over its opponents when it first appeared in action in 1941 was countered by the Germans with the introduction of the Panther and Tiger, and by up-gunning the PzKpfw IV. Nevertheless, successive improvements in the armament and protection of the T-34 kept it in the forefront of medium tanks throughout the rest of the war.

These improvements were accompanied by various other changes, although the main basic features of the T-34's design were retained throughout its long life. All this was achieved without undue interruption to the production flow although it led to many transitional models. The Russians did not allocate model numbers at all but the main differences between T-34 variants were, however, classified by the Western Allies and the Germans, and the model letters they allotted have been used here.

The original production version of the T-34, the T-34/76A, as it became known outside the Soviet Union, had a turret design which was unsatisfactory in some respects. This was replaced in the T-34/76B by a new turret incorporating a 76·2-mm. gun with a length of 41·2 calibres (compared with the earlier gun's 30·5 calibres) and increased muzzle velocity. Vision arrangements were improved and the 'pig's head' type of mantlet was replaced by a bolted one of more angular shape in which the gun was mounted relatively higher. (This incidentally resulted in the depression of the gun being no more than 4 degrees, one of the weaker points of the T-34's design, but accepted because one solution—raising the height of the turret roof—would have increased vulnerability). The earlier turrets of Model B were of rolled plate, welded, but during 1942 a cast version was introduced and this pattern is shown in the illustration.

Good as it was, it became necessary to increase the hitting power of the T-34 and during the summer of 1943, A. A. Morozov, who had taken over as chief designer from M. I. Koshkin, who died in 1940, redesigned the tank to accept a new turret armed with an 85-mm. gun. The gun was an adaptation of a pre-war anti-aircraft gun and was in a turret designed for the KV-85 heavy tank, so, once more, introducing standardization between the two classes of Russian tank. Later, though, this turret was re-designed and the second model of the T-34/85, using the new turret is shown in the illustration in this book.

The T-34/85's roomier turret enabled a five-man crew to be used and the protection was increased to a maximum of 75-mm. at the front. The main essentials of all T-34s remained, however, including the V-12 cylinder diesel engine of 500 h.p. driving rear sprockets and the Christie suspension of large road wheels on pivot arms controlled by long coil springs. Although many improvements had been introduced since 1940, the T-34 was still basically a simple and rugged but effective design, well suited to mass production. Nearly 40,000 T-34s of all types were built during World War II.

74 KV-85 (Heavy Tank) and SU-85, U.S.S.R.

The need to improve the armament of the KV-1 heavy tank was emphasized during the great battle of Kursk in 1943, in which the Soviet tanks encountered the German Tiger tanks in appreciable numbers. The 85-mm. gun in a new turret was fitted to the KV-1 in that year and the first of the new tanks, designated KV-85, were in action by the Autumn of 1943. The new combination was roughly equivalent to the German Tiger I (although more lightly armoured) and the Russians took the opportunity of reworking existing KV-1s to the new standard in order to make available quickly larger numbers of tanks capable of taking on the Tiger on equal terms. By Russian standards only small numbers of KV-85s were built—but the design was used as the basis of the Stalin tank which succeeded the KV series.

Roughly at the time the KV-85 appeared in service in 1943 and when a heavy tank with a more powerful gun than the 85-mm. was already envisaged, the SU-85 was designed. This SU (the initials stand for Samachodnya Ustanovka—self-propelled [gun] mounting) was intended as a 'tank hunter' and carried the high velocity 85-mm. gun in a mounting with limited traverse in a low (and hence less conspicuous) well-armoured hull on the T-34 chassis. This device, of using a standard (or, sometimes, obsolescent) chassis to to mount a heavier gun and, at the same time, achieve better protection and/or mobility than with the same weapon on a tank, was widely used by the Germans in World War II.

Often used in conjunction with T-34/76s, the SU-85 was in production from about the end of 1943 for about a year, when it gradually began to be replaced by the SU-100, with a more powerful gun, which used the same chassis and which was similar in appearance. Another widely used self-propelled gun on the T-34 chassis was the SU-122, a 122-mm. low velocity howitzer, which was in service from early 1943 onwards.

75 JS-II (Heavy Tank), U.S.S.R.

The Josef Stalin or JS-II heavy tank with its long 122-mm. gun was one of the most powerful tanks to go into service with any army in World War II.

A tank which traced its ancestry directly back to the KV series, the JS-II was another product of the design team headed by General Z. A. Kotin. Taking the KV-85 as a base, the best points were retained but others, including the suspension and transmission, were redesigned. A two-stage planetary transmission, combined with an improved engine led to better manœuvrability and overall performance. At the same time, the opportunity was taken of rearranging the internal layout in a more compact form, allowing for armour increases while decreasing the total weight compared with KV-85.

The earliest JS tanks had the same 85-mm. gun as the KV. This was then replaced by a 100-mm. weapon and then, finally, by the 122-mm. gun. As this gun needed a wider turret ring, the hull at that point had to be extended out over the tracks each side but to avoid increasing the height, the top run of the track was lowered, although in most other respects the torsion bar suspension of the JS was similar to that of the KV's.

Known as JS-I or JS-122, the first 122-mm. gun-armed Stalin tanks entered service in late 1943. The JS-II which followed was generally similar but had the hull redesigned to give greater protection, notably in the better slope on the glacis plate.

The 122-mm. gun on the JS-II had a 7·62-mm. machine-gun as a coaxial weapon. The tank was served by a crew of four. The combat weight was 45 tons and with a 600-b.h.p. twelve-cylinder-V diesel engine had a top speed of 23 m.p.h. Armour was at a maximum thickness of 120-mm.

Over 2,000 JS-IIs were produced during the war, before being superseded by even the better JS-III, which became one of the most formidable tanks of the post-war years.

76 JSU-122 and JSU-152, U.S.S.R.

Two powerful self-propelled guns based on the Stalin heavy tank chassis, the JSU-122 and JSU-152 both entered service in 1944. Superseding similar weapons mounted on the earlier KV chassis (known as SU-122 and SU-152) to which they bore a strong resemblance, these two self-propelled guns had a better mechanical performance and, among other detail improvements, improved fire control arrangements.

The 122-mm. gun used in the earlier JSU-122s (one of which is shown in the illustration) was 45 calibres long and had a range of over 14,000 yards. Later models had a 43-calibre gun with a muzzle brake. The 152-mm. gun (29 calibres long) of the JSU-152 was a howitzer with a range of well over 9,000 yards. The ammunition (weighing 96 lb for high explosive and 107 lb per round for armour piercing) was so bulky, however, that only twenty rounds could be carried.

Carrying a crew of four (five if the vehicle was fitted with radio) the two JSUs were mechanically the same as their heavy tank counterparts and had much the same performance. This was important, because they were generally employed integrally with heavy tank regiments equipped with JS tanks.

77 KT (Winged Tank) and SU-76 U.S.S.R.

By the end of 1942, the Russians were already beginning to regard light tanks as a class as obsolete and although the type was developed from the T-40 of 1941 through the T-60 and T-70 to the T-80 of 1943, production of light tanks was tailed off in that year and had ceased before the war ended. At one time regarded mainly for their amphibious qualities, the Russians also gave some consideration to the potential of the light tank as an airborne vehicle. One of the most interesting tank experiments by any country in World War II was the Russian design for a Kyrliatyi Tank (KT) or 'winged tank'.

This design, by a team led by O. Antonov, consisted of a T-60 light tank, more or less in standard form, to which biplane wings, twin booms and a tail assembly were attached. These aerodynamic structures were made of wood, mainly, it seems, because of the shortage of aircraft alloys for experi-

ments of this kind. Rudimentary flying controls were led from the wings and tail to the tank, which formed the 'fuselage' of the machine.

The first test flight took place in 1942 and was curtailed only because of a fault in the engines of the towing aircraft. The winged tank apparently performed satisfactorily, but eventually the project had to be cancelled because of a shortage of the four-engined towing aircraft that would have been needed in some quantity to justify production of the tank gliders.

The T-60 light tank, as used in this experiment, was a 6-ton vehicle armed with a 20-mm. gun and a 7·62-mm. machine-gun. Maximum armour protection was 20-mm. and a 70-b.h.p. GAZ—202 six-cylinder petrol engine gave the tank a top speed of about 27 m.p.h.

The successor to the T-60 light tank was the T-70, which weighed 9 tons and had a 45-mm. gun and 7·62-mm. machine-gun. Several thousand were produced in 1942–43. Before production ceased, however, it had already been decided to utilize the T-70 chassis as the basis of a self-propelled mounting for the 76·2-mm. anti-tank gun.

The vehicle which emerged, the SU-76, used automotive and running gear similar to that of the T-70, although an extra road wheel each side was added to accommodate the longer hull needed as a self-propelled mounting. The power unit, mounted at the right-hand side of the hull, consisted of two engines, GAZ-202 of 70-b.h.p. each in earlier vehicles and GAZ-203 of 85-b.h.p. each in late production vehicles. Independent torsion bars for each road wheel were used for the suspension. The 76·2-mm. gun, 41·5 calibres long, was mounted at the rear in an open-topped compartment with a total traverse of 32 degrees. The relatively light armour and absence of overhead protection made the SU-76 less suitable as an anti-tank vehicle once the gun began to be outranged by more powerful German weapons. It was replaced by the SU-85 as an anti-tank vehicle, therefore, and switched to the infantry support role.

The SU-76 shown in the illustration is one of the earlier production vehicles.

78 BA-64 (Light Armoured Car), U.S.S.R.

Armoured car development in the Soviet Union in World War II was very limited indeed because, apart from improvements to the two main pre-war designs, only one new model appeared. This was the BA-64, which went into production in 1942. A light armoured scout car with 4-wheel drive, said to have been inspired by the German SdKfz 222, to which it bore a slight resemblance, the BA-64 had a crew of two—the driver and the commander, who had a small open top multi-sided turret equipped with a machine-gun. This was normally a 7·62-mm. weapon, mounted in the turret face, or on top for anti-aircraft use, but alternatively a heavy 14·5-mm. machine-gun on a pintle mount could be carried.

Weighing about 2½ tons, the BA-64 was powered by a four-cylinder 50-b.h.p. GAZ petrol engine, which gave it a maximum speed of 31 m.p.h.

79 Tanque 'Narhuel', Modelo DL 43, Argentina.

Designed in Argentina in 1943 and produced in that country, the 'Narhuel' was a medium tank weighing 35 tons. The name 'Narhuel' is a South American Indian name for the jaguar. Although owing much in inspiration and configuration to the United States M.4 Medium, the 'Narhuel' was otherwise entirely original in design. The main armament consisted of a 75-mm. gun. A machine-gun was mounted coaxially with the 75-mm. gun on the left side and there were up to three others in the hull glacis plate, with another for anti-aircraft use.

The crew consisted of five men and with a 500-h.p. engine the maximum speed was 25 m.p.h. and the range was about 150 miles. The maximum armour protection was 80-mm.

Only sixteen of these tanks were built, the need for further production of medium tanks in Argentina ceasing to exist after 1944 when supplies of U.S. M.4 mediums and other equipment became available.

80 Stridsvagn M/42 and Storm-artillerivagn M/43, Sweden.

Swedish armoured fighting vehicle development during World War II followed a policy of steady progress in mechanical improvement and up-gunning, as far as was possible with the resources available.

The 22½-ton Strv. M/42, designed by Landsverk, had a family resemblance to that concern's earlier, much lighter, series taken into Swedish Army service as Strv. M/38, M/39 and M/40. The latter were armed only with 37-mm. guns, however, which by 1942 were inadequate, and it was decided to adopt a short calibre 75-mm. gun for the Strv. M/42. With a crew of four and armour protection to an 80-mm. maximum, the Strv. M/42 was powered by an eight-cylinder Volvo water-cooled engine developing 380 b.h.p. which produced a top speed of 29 m.p.h. Two 8-mm. machine-guns were mounted to the right of the 75-mm. gun in the turret and a third machine gun was in the front of the hull.

In 1945 the Strv. M/42 was re-designated Infanterikanonvagn 73 (Ikv 73) to reflect the new role for this tank as an infantry support vehicle.

The Stormartillerivagn M/43 (Sav. M/43), which appeared in 1944, used the chassis of the Czech-designed LT-38 built under licence in Sweden by Scania-Vavis A.B. as Stridsvagn M/41. This assault gun mounted a 10·5-cm. howitzer in a fixed, enclosed armoured superstructure. Weighing 12 tons and with a crew of four, the Sav. M/43 had a six-cylinder Scania-Vabis engine of 140 b.h.p., which gave it a maximum speed of about 27 m.p.h. The Strv. M/41 design, on which the Sav. M/43 was based, had a very long life for a fighting vehicle, incidentally, because in 1962 chassis of this type were rebuilt as armoured personnel carriers.

APPENDIX

Armoured Fighting Vehicle Camouflage and Markings 1942-45

The artist in conjunction with the author has tried to show camouflage colours as they are likely to have appeared, and tactical and other markings for specific vehicles have been included where practicable. However, in some cases, information has been unobtainable or incomplete: black and white photographs, for example, are an unreliable guide as to whether a vehicle is painted a medium brown or medium green colour. Even reproductions of colour photo transparencies are often very misleading—for example, one photograph in colour of a Churchill tank which was reproduced in a journal showed it as something very much like middle bronze green, whereas the original transparency, which the author has examined, proves that the tank in question was actually khaki brown!

Apart from the difficulties of colour reproduction in a book, the colours used on the actual vehicles often varied for many reasons—the exact colours for camouflage were not always considered important and wide discretion was allowed to unit and tank commanders; the quality control on paints issued—always difficult to maintain—sometimes allowed quite wide variations; and colours, once applied, could sometimes be changed out of all recognition by ageing, frequently helped by terrain such as desert sand. References to official colour standard specifications are given below in some cases and these are the surest basis of information available today on exact shades as they were supposed to be applied. Even so, allowance has to be made for variations from causes such as those mentioned above and it must always be borne in mind that, for example, a dark colour, particularly in bright sunlight, will appear much lighter when spread over a wide surface and, of course, the reverse applies to a light colour in deep shadow.

For those wishing to pursue the subject, useful articles discussing the problems involved as well as details of actual colour schemes have appeared in the journals *Tankette* and *A.F.V. News*, details of which are given in the Foreword.

Argentina

The colour for fighting vehicles was either plain olive green or, where necessary, a three-colour disruptive pattern of olive green, brown and dark green.

Australia

Camouflage and markings were on similar lines to those used by the United Kingdom except that for A.F.V.s in Australia itself a two- or three-colour scheme using shades better matching the local terrain was used. For operations in New Guinea and Borneo, tanks were painted 'Jungle green'—a very dark green.

Tactical signs were as for the United Kingdom, except that independent squadrons used an inverted triangle symbol.

Canada

See under United Kingdom.

France (Fighting France)

Vehicles in the Western Desert were usually sand colour, as for contemporary British vehicles. Original French vehicles had French registration numbers, vehicles supplied by the British usually carried the original W.D. numbers. When American equipment was provided in the Italian campaign and for use in France itself in 1944–45, U.S. camouflage colours (usually olive drab) were used.

Germany

In 1942 grey, ranging from medium to dark was in general use, except in North Africa where sand yellow was normally used. A mottled pattern of green or brown was sometimes added in North Africa, more often in Tunisia near the end of the campaign.

An order dated 18 February 1943 instructed that all A.F.V.s leaving the factories should be finished in a standard dark sand (yellow) colour, although in 1944, perhaps due to paint shortages, some vehicles again left the factories in a grey finish. Tank crews in the field were issued with a supply of paint (diluted with water or petrol before use) for each vehicle—usually reddish-brown, olive drab and dark yellow—so that a camouflage pattern appropriate to the terrain could be added to the basic colour.

Thus the degree of dilution of the paint applied in the field and/or the skill and whims of the crews resulted in a very wide range of colours and patterns in German A.F.V. camouflage. A German expert has said that exceptions to the rule were very common. The German black cross, on hull and/or turret sides and rear, outlined in white, was shown on most A.F.V.s.

The basic colours used were allotted RAL numbers by the department responsible for paint standards and although a full list is not available, some of these were as follows (an asterisk following the number denotes that the colour is still a published standard in West Germany in 1975)—RAL 6006* (dark green), RAL 6007* (medium-dark green), RAL 7016* (very dark bluish-grey), RAL 7017 (very dark brownish grey), RAL 7021* (very dark grey), RAL 8002 (khaki-brown), RAL 8020 (dark cream).

A tactical number was usually carried on most German A.F.V.s, although more often omitted on armoured cars and half-tracks. This number was usually in black or red, outlined in white, or sometimes in white or white outline only. The system for allocating these numbers was usually as follows, although there were exceptions to the general rule.

R 01	regimental commander
R 02	regimental adjutant
R 03	ordnance or signals officer
R 04 etc.	regimental staff etc.
I 01	commander of I battalion
I 02	adjutant of I battalion
I 03	ordnance officer of I battalion
I 04	staff of I battalion
II 01 etc.	commander of II battalion etc.
101	officer commanding Ist company, I battalion
102	2nd in command 1st company I battalion
111	Leader, 1st platoon, 1st company, I battalion
112	2nd vehicle, 1st platoon, 1st company, I battalion
133	3rd vehicle, 3rd platoon, I battalion
201 etc.	officer commanding 2nd company
301–801 etc.	Panzer battalions consisted of three or four companies and the above system was continued up to 801 etc. for the 8th company of the II battalion.
901 1001 1101 etc.	Tiger battalion of a special Panzer division, such as the 'Grossdeutschland' in 1944. Also independent Tiger or Sturmgeschütz company (9th) of some divisions or reconnaisance companies (10th and 11th) in others.

The system included even higher serials in some special cases. Only the final digit, denoting the individual vehicle in the platoon, was used in some instances.

A battery letter (in plain or Gothic letters) was sometimes carried on self-propelled guns, denoting the battery to which the vehicle belonged.

Small symbolic signs indicating the type of unit and the sub-unit within that unit were carried on some armoured vehicles, but not often on tanks.

Small divisional signs, usually in yellow, but white or black was also used, were sometimes stencilled on A.F.V. hulls or turrets.

Vehicle registration serial numbers, prefixed by WH for the Army, by the double lightning flash for the SS, and WL for the Luftwaffe (e.g. Hermann Göring Division) were carried on armoured cars and half tracks but not on full tracked A.F.V.s. The letters/numbers were in black on a white background.

India

See under United Kingdom.

Italy

Sand yellow, with or without a darker disruptive pattern, in North Africa; dark greenish-grey in Europe, with sometimes a shadowy or sharp reticulated pattern added.

Tactical markings consisted firstly of the regimental number in white arabic figures and the battalion number in white Roman figures. These were usually carried on rear surfaces of the tank's fighting compartment. Battalion command tanks were denoted on the turret or hull by a rectangle divided vertically into red, blue and yellow strips or, where there were only two companies in the battalion, red and blue only. The company signs, carried on the sides and rear of the turret (or hull, in turretless vehicles) were as follows:

1st company—red rectangle
2nd company—blue rectangle
3rd company—yellow rectangle
4th company—green rectangle

Platoons were indicated by one, two or three vertical white bars on the company sign, indicating 1st, 2nd or 3rd platoon respectively. The position of the individual tank in the platoon was shown by an arabic number in white or the company colour above or below the company sign.

These markings were generally used in Africa, less frequently so in Europe.

A vehicle registration number was usually carried at front and rear. The number was in black on a white background, preceded by RoEto (Regio Esercito = Royal Army) in red.

Japan

A three-colour camouflage scheme was generally used, consisting of a sand (yellow) colour, brown and dark green, although dark green alone also appeared.

Tactical signs were not standardized and were used only in some units. Sometimes these consisted of large Western figures in white on hull or turret, with or without Japanese characters. A red sun symbol, with or without the rays, sometimes was used and appeared on turret, nose plates or front mudguards of tanks. A yellow star was sometimes embossed or painted on the glacis plate of tanks.

Registration plates, when carried on tanks, appeared on the rear plate of the hull only. These showed a white star, Japanese characters and a number in Western figures.

Jordan

Arab Legion armoured cars were a mustard colour to which sometimes a disruptive pattern was added. British-style geometric tactical signs were sometimes carried. The vehicle number usually appeared in both Western and Arabic figures on the mudguards on opposite sides.

South Africa

See under United Kingdom.

Sweden

A camouflage system of grey, brown, green and black, in patches. In winter, vehicles were overpainted in white.

A small reproduction of the Swedish flag was generally carried on A.F.V.s after 1941.

Large tactical numbers in black, outlined, were sometimes carried on A.F.V.s, including armoured cars.

U.S.S.R.

Russian tanks were usually painted in a single colour of green or brown shade. Sometimes, but only infrequently, a disruptive pattern in a dark shade was added. A.F.V.s in winter were frequently painted over in white.

Sometimes (but rarely in combat) a red star was shown on the turret or hull. Slogans—generally of a patriotic nature—were rather more frequently shown on tanks in combat. Call signs, usually painted in white (black on snow-camouflaged vehicles) and enclosed in geometric shapes, often came increasingly to be shown. Large white numbers on turrets or hulls of A.F.Vs were also sometimes shown towards the end of the war.

British A.F.V.s in the United Kingdom at the beginning of 1942 were permitted to be painted in a basic colour of either a shade of dark green, Middle Bronze Green (British Standards Institution specification No. 381—1930, colour No. 23 or B.S.I. 987c Shade No. 7) or a khaki brown colour, known as Standard Camouflage Colour No. 2 (published in B.S.I. No. 987c—1942). Khaki brown predominated, however, and appeared also in various lighter shades, including Shade No. 4 in B.S.I. 987c—1942. Nevertheless, several Regimental histories of British armoured regiments in the Eighth Army refer to the dark green of the First Army vehicles (newly out from the United Kingdom) encountered in Tunisia in 1943 or of repainting their own desert-camouflaged vehicles in green for the forthcoming campaign in Italy.

If a dark disruptive colour was to be added to either the green or the brown basic colour, the War Office instructed that this was to be the very dark brown known as Standard Camouflage Colour No. 1A (also published in B.S.I. 987c—1942).

In 1944, a new instruction laid down that the brown Standard Camouflage Colour No. 2 should be replaced by olive drab, officially known as Shade No. 15, an amendment to B.S.I. 987c—1942. This colour was much like the green used in 1942 but somewhat duller. It was similar to the U.S. Army standard 'olive drab'. Also in 1944, the use of a dark disruptive colour was no longer authorized.

British armoured fighting vehicles in North Africa (except those of the First Army in Tunisia) were painted in various sand colours, ranging from yellow through various stone-coloured shades to pink. To these were added, when required, various darker disruptive shades. In some regiments with cruiser tanks with large road wheels, the inner wheels were painted black to make them 'disappear' and so cause the tank to look more like a lorry—an effect heightened by the use of 'sun shields' (canvas on iron hoops) to conceal the turret and upper surfaces.

Armoured fighting vehicles of British and Indian formations in Burma were painted 'jungle green'. This was, contrary to some belief, a very dark colour, an olive drab darker than that used in Europe. In 1942 it would have been Shade No. 13 in B.S.I. 987c—1942, replaced in 1945 by Shade No. 16, 'Very Dark Drab'. Australian tanks in New Guinea and Borneo were also painted in a dark 'jungle green'.

Formation signs were carried by British A.F.V.s, normally at the front and rear of the hull. All British units were allotted a unit code sign, usually applicable to the type of unit, which was often unique *only* in conjunction with the formation sign. The code sign was a white number on a coloured square. Code numbers were usually allocated to armoured regiments in the brigade in accordance with their seniority in the Army List. The main exception to these rules were signals units which had the code number in red on a square divided horizontally white over blue. The code numbers used were of those of the headquarters of the formation served by the signals unit.

The most important of these unit code numbers for A.F.V.s in Armoured Divisions in 1942–45 were as follows:

	Europe 1942–45	Libya 1942
Armoured Division Headquarters	40	49
Headquarters (I) Armoured Brigade	50	71
Armoured Regiment (Battalion) (1)	51	40
Armoured Regiment (Battalion) (2)	52	86
Armoured Regiment (Battalion) (3)	53	67
Headquarters (II) Armoured Brigade (a)	60	
Armoured Regiment (Battalion) (1)	61	
Armoured Regiment (Battalion) (2)	62	
Armoured Regiment (Battalion) (3)	63	
Armoured Car Regiment (b)	44	76
Armoured Reconnaissance Regiment (c)	45	

Notes

(a) The second armoured brigade was deleted during the course of 1942 although in North Africa, divisions still often had two or even three armoured brigades on an *ad hoc* basis. These extra brigades sometimes had the same unit code numbers as the (I) brigade, although they were usually distinguished by their brigade signs.

(b) At first 47 in the United Kingdom. Deleted from armoured divisions to become Corps Troops in 1943, but restored in 1945.

(c) Added to armoured division in 1943.

The coloured squares for the unit code signs were black for Divisional Headquarters, red for Headquarters and units of (I) Brigade, and green for Headquarters and units of (II) Brigade. The unit code numbers of the latter, incidentally, were taken over by the Lorried Infantry Brigades after the 1942 reorganization. For armoured car regiments the colours varied, although at first black in the U.K. and finally, in 1945, as for Armoured Reconnaissance Regiments, namely blue and green, divided horizontally.

Independent tank brigades and armoured brigades used various code-sign numbers (155, 156, 157 for the three tank units of the 34th Tank Brigade in 1944 for example) although the numbers were standardized as 51, 52, 53 (as in the armoured divisions) by 1945. White bars to denote allocation to a higher formation—above the code sign for Corps Troops, below the sign for Army Troops, and diagonally for Army Group—were added as appropriate.

Tactical signs were standardized by 1942 as the following hollow geometric shapes, painted on turrets and/or hulls, as follows:

Regimental (Battalion) Headquarters—diamond
'A' Squadron (Company)—triangle
'B' Squadron (Company)—square
'C' Squadron (Company)—circle
'D' Squadron (Company)—vertical bar

Canadian units sometimes used an inverted triangle for 'A' Squadron.

These tactical signs were in the following colours:

Senior Regiment in Brigade—red
Second Regiment in Brigade—yellow
Third Regiment in Brigade—blue
Fourth Regiment in Brigade—green

In armoured formations, only armoured car regiments or infantry motor battalions had a fourth squadron or company and the fourth unit in an armoured brigade was usually the motor battalion. From about 1943 onwards some British armoured regiments adopted a numbering system to supplement or replace the tactical signs. Large serial numbers were shown on hull or turret sides and rear. Unlike the German system, this did not denote battalion, company and platoon but ran through the unit, the order differing between regiments, although pains were usually taken to avoid numbering regimental headquarters tanks with the lowest numbers, and thus make them stand out.

British A.F.V.s frequently carried individual names, usually allocated in associated groups for squadrons and/or sub units, and/or bearing the same initial letter as the squadron letter. They were often names associated with regimental tradition or links, such as battle honours, recruiting towns or districts. In the battalions of the Royal Tank Regiment, the World War I tradition of naming all tanks with a letter equivalent to the battalion number (e.g. 4th Battalion tank names—Destroyer, Devil, Duck etc.) was continued in World War II.

The War Department registration number (prefixed by T for tanks, F for armoured cars, and so on) was carried in white (or black for light-painted vehicles) on the front and rear of the hull and/or hull or turret sides, according to the type of vehicle.

Varying A.F.V. recognition signs were used at different times. The white/red/white strips adopted in the Middle East in late 1941 were abandoned about March 1942 to be followed by a white St Andrew's cross on upper surfaces (principally for air recognition) and then in turn by R.A.F.-type roundels (blue, white and red—the latter in the centre). In the United Kingdom, red/white/red strips were painted on A.F.V.s in March 1942 as a recognition sign and this applied also to the First Army vehicles in Tunisia and was later used in Italy until mid-1943. The white five-pointed star (with or without an enclosing ring) first used by American forces in the North African landings in 1942 was adopted by the War Office for general use as an 'Allied Star' by British forces in June 1943. Usually shown on top surfaces as an air recognition sign, it also appeared sometimes on hull or turret sides, particularly on tanks in the Far East.

Finally, a bridge group number was usually carried by British A.F.V.s. This denoted the maximum loaded weight of the vehicle in tons and the figure was in black on a yellow disc or within a yellow ring, shown at the front.

U.S.A.

The most common basic colour finish for U.S. A.F.V.s was green, although the shade varied widely. In 1942, however, the dark green commonly used (U.S. Army Ref. No. 320, similar to the British B.S.I. 987c—1942, shade No. 7) was generally superseded for Army vehicles by olive drab (Ref. No. 319). A range of other basic colours, suited to different terrains, was available, though, and recommended styles of application of darker disruptive patterns (in one or two colours) were published by the U.S. War Department. The U.S. Marine Corps also came to use olive drab as the basic colour, although forest green (a colour not dissimilar to olive drab but less brown) was standard. Landing Vehicles Tracked were sometimes finished in naval grey. Disruptive patterns, sometimes somewhat bizarre, were used, but not consistently.

A system of tactical signs including full details from formation down to company level was introduced in 1943. This consisted of small white numbers, symbols and letters, carried at front and rear, of which 7 △ 31 △ B-13 is an example, denoting 7th Armored Division, 31st Armored Battalion, B company, 13th vehicle (actually a Sherman tank). (In the Cavalry, the signs represented squadron and troop, and in the Artillery battalion and battery.) Prior to this, only the Company and vehicle designator was usually shown (sometimes in conjunction with the divisional sign, though), but even late in the war, where security necessitated it, other symbols were painted out leaving only the company and vehicle sign. The U.S. 1st Armored Division in Tunisia in 1942 used a permutated system of white geometric shapes denoting battalion, company and platoon, with a number added to indicate the individual tank.

United States Marine Corps vehicles sometimes carried geometric shapes (diamond, semi-circle, rectangle etc.) surrounding a number indicating regiment, battalion and company. Tactical letters and numbers or larger numbers alone also were used on A.F.V. hulls and/or turrets.

Vehicle registration letters were shown in white or pale blue prefixed by 'USA' (for Army vehicles) usually, on tanks, on the hull sides near the rear. The first digits were standardized for the type, tanks always having 30 (e.g. USA 3031428—an M.4 Medium tank), half tracks and tracked vehicles except tanks (such as S.P. guns) —40; armoured cars—60; tracked tractors (including L.V.T.s)—9. U.S. Marine Corps vehicles did not conform to this system and carried the prefix 'U.S.M.C.'.

The general recognition sign of a five-pointed star was used by the U.S. forces from 1942 onwards. This was normally white, with or without a white outer ring.

The bridge group sign of a black figure (denoting the maximum laden weight in tons) on a yellow disc was often carried at the front of U.S. armoured vehicles in Europe.

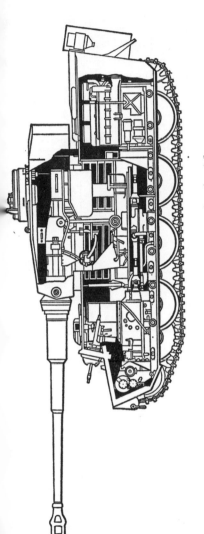

Panzerkampfwagen VI, Tiger I, Germany — length 20′4″

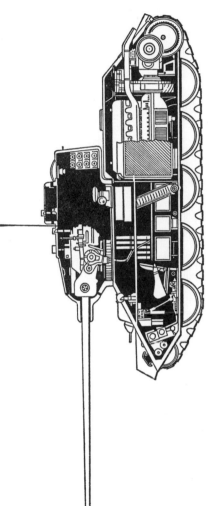

T-34/85 (Medium Tank), U.S.S.R. — length 19′8″

The dimensions and weights given here should be taken as a rough guide only: in some cases they
tions. Most of the specialized armoured vehicles are not included in these tables, because in most cases
the standard vehicles from which they have been developed and due allowance has to be made for the
Gun calibre lengths are not shown here but these should always be taken into account (and als
ment' column, 'm.g.' has been used to denote machine-guns of rifle calibre and 'h.m.g.' for weapo

FULL-TRACKED

Ref. No.	Type	Weight tons	Length ft in.		Width ft in.		Height ft in.		Armour max. mm.	Armament
	Japan									
1	Tankette, Type 97	4·25	12	0	5	11	5	10	12	1 37-mm.
1	Light, Type 95	7·50	14	1	6	11	7	3	12	1 37-mm., 2 m.g.
2	Medium, Type 97 (new turret)	15·80	18	1	7	8	7	11	25	1 47-mm., 2m.g.
2	Medium Type 3	19·00	18	6	7	8	8	7	50	1 75-mm., 2 m.g.
3	Medium Type 4	30·00	20	9	9	5	9	5	75	1 75-mm., 2 m.g.
3	Medium, Type 5	37·00	24	0	10	0	10	0	75	1 75-mm., 1 37-mm 2 m.g.
5	Amphibious, Type 2	12·50	24	7	9	2	7	6	12	1 37-mm., 2 m.g.
5	Amphibious, Type 3	28·80	33	9	9	10	12	6	50	1 47-mm., 2 m.g.
8	Armoured Personnel Carrier, Type 1	6·5	15	1	6	11	8	3	6	—
	U.S.A.									
9	Light M.5A1	15·13	15	10	7	6	7	10	67	1 37-mm., 3 m.g.
10	Light M.22	7·32	12	11	7	4	5	8	25	1 37-mm., 1 m.g.
10	Light M.24	18·08	18	0	9	4	8	1	63	1 75-mm., 3 m.g.
11	Medium M.3	26·80	18	6	8	11	10	3	51	1 75-mm., 1 37-mm 3 m.g.
12	Medium M.4	29·69	19	4	8	7	9	0	51	1 75-mm., 1 m.g.
13	Medium M.26	41·52	20	9	11	6	9	1	102	1 90-mm., 3 m.g.
14	Heavy M.6	56·48	24	9	10	2	9	10	82	1 3-in.., 1 37-mm., 4 m.g.
9	75-mm. H.M.C. M.8	15·44	14	7	7	4	7	6	44	1 75-mm., 3 m.g.
15	105-mm. H.M.C. M.7	22·60	19	9	9	5	8	4	62	1 105-mm., 1 m.g.
16	3-in. G.M.C. M.10	29·46	19	7	10	0	8	1	63	1 3-in., 1 m.g.
16	76-mm. G.M.C. M.18	16·80	17	10	9	5	8	5	25	1 76-mm., 1 m.g.
17	L.V.T.(A)4	18·30	26	2	10	8	10	2	13	1 75-mm.
17	L.V.T. 4	16·25	26	1	10	8	8	1	—	1 m.g.
	U.K., Canada and Australia									
21	Tetrarch	7·50	13	6	7	7	6	11	16	1 2-pr, 1 m.g.
21	Harry Hopkins	8·50	14	3	8	10	6	11	38	1 2-pr, 1 m.g.
22	Crusader I	19·00	19	8	8	8	7	4	40	1 2-pr, 2 m.g.
22	Crusader III	19·75	19	8	8	8	7	4	51	1 6-pr, 1 m.g.
23	Centaur IV	27·50	20	10	9	6	8	2	76	1 95-mm. how, 1 1
23	Cromwell	28·00	20	10	10	0	8	2	76	1 75-mm. or 6-pr., 2 m.g.
24	Challenger	31·50	26	4	9	6	8	9	102	1 17-pr, 1 m.g.
25	Comet	32·50	21	6	10	0	8	9	101	1 77-mm., 2 m.g.
26	Ram II (Canada)	29·50	19	0	9	10	8	9	76	1 6-pr, 2 m.g.
27	Aust. Cruiser A.C.I	28·00	20	9	9	1	8	5	65	1 2-pr, 2 m.g.
28	Churchill III	39·00	24	5	10	8	9	0	102	1 6-pr, 2 m.g.
28	Churchill VII	40·00	24	5	11	4	9	0	152	1 75-mm., 2 m.g.
29	Bishop	17·20	18	2	8	7	9	1	60	1 25-pr
29	Archer	16·00	21	11	9	0	7	4	60	1 17-pr
30	Sexton (Canada)	25·4	19	3	8	11	8	0	32	1 25-pr
37	Carrier, Universal Mk II	3·95	12	4	6	11	5	3	12	1 m.g.
37	Aust. 2-pr Carrier	5·15	13	11	6	10	6	5	12	1 2-pr
	Italy									
50	M.15/42	15	16	7	7	4	7	9	42	1 47-mm., 2 m.g.
51	P.40	25	18	8	9	1	8	3	50	1 75-mm., 2 m.g.
52	Semovente 75/34	15	16	7	7	3	6	1	42	1 75-mm., 1 m.g.
52	Semovente 105/23	15·7	16	8	7	11	5	9	50	1 105-mm., 1 m.g.

oximations. Performance figures are also approximate—they can vary widely under different condi-
ot lend themselves to tabular description. However, their basic characteristics are similar to those of
erformance of the special equipment carried.
ion of the weapon) when comparing guns of the same calibre (i.e. diameter of the bore). In the 'arma-
nd 12–15 mm., but below 20-mm.

OURED VEHICLES

Engine	b.h.p.	Speed m.p.h.	Range miles	Crew	Notes
ii diesel	65	26	155	2	
bishi diesel	110	28	155	3	
97 diesel	170	24	130	4	
100 diesel	240	25	130	5	
4 diesel	400	28	155	5	
W. (petrol)	550	28	125	5	
bishi diesel	110	23	200	5	Water speed 6 m.p.h.
100 diesel	240	20	200	7	Water speed 6 m.p.h.
	134	25	—	15	
ac	220	40	100	4	
ning	162	35	110	3	
ac	220	35	175	5	
nental	340	26	120	6	Grant, height 9 ft 4 in.
inental	400	24	120	5	
	470	20	75	5	
it	800	22	100	6	
ac	220	40	100	4	
nental	340	25	105	7	
al Motors	375	30	200	5	Length including gun 21 ft 10 in.
nental	340/400	55	105	5	Water: speed 7 m.p.h., range 100 miles.
nental	250	16	150	6	Water: speed 7·5 m.p.h., range 75 miles.
nental	250	20	150	7	
ows	165	40	140	3	2-pr gun = calibre 40-mm.
ows	148	30	125	3	
eld Liberty	340	27	100	5	6-pr gun = calibre 57 mm.
eld Liberty	340	27	100	3	
eld Liberty	395	27	165	5	
Royce	600	32	165	5	17-pr gun = calibre 76-mm.
Royce	600	32	105	5	Length including gun 25 ft 1 in.
Royce	600	29	123	5	
nental	400	25	144	5	
ac (× 3)	330	30	200	5	
rd	350	15·5	90	5	
rd	350	12·5	90	5	
. diesel	131	15	90	4	
al Motors diesel	192	20	140	4	
nental	400	25	180	6	484 b.h.p. engine on some
	85	32	160	4–5	
	95	20	160	4	
	190	25	140	4	
	330	25	175	4	
	190	25	140	3	
	190	24	95	3	

Ref. No.	Type	Weight tons	Length ft in.	Width ft in.	Height ft in.	Armour max. mm.	Armament
	Germany						
53	PzKpfw. Luchs	11·8	14 6	8 2	7 0	30	1 2-cm., 1 m.g.
54	PzKpfw. III, Ausf. L-M	21·95	18 1	9 8	8 3	50+20	1 5-cm., 2 m.g.
55	PzKpfw IV, Ausf. H.	24·61	19 4	10 8	8 10	80	1 7·5-cm., 2 m.g.
56	PzKpfw Panther (Ausf. G)	44·10	22 7	11 3	9 10	80	1 7·5-cm., 2 m.g.
57	PzKpfw Tiger I	54·13	20 4	12 3	9 5	100	1 8·8-cm., 2 m.g.
58	PzKpfw Tiger II	68·6	23 10	12 4	10 2	150	1 8·8-cm., 2 m.g.
59	PzKpfw Maus	185	29 8	12 1	12 0	200	1 15-cm., 1 7·5-cm. 1 m.g.
59	PzKpfw E.100	137·79	28 6	14 8	10 11	200	1 15-cm., 1 7·5-cm. 1 m.g.
60	JgPz 38(t) Hetzer	15·75	16 0	8 8	6 11	60	1 7·5-cm., 1 m.g.
61	Stu. G. III/10·5 cm. Stu.H.	23·52	18 4	9 9	7 0	50+30	1 10·5-cm., 1 m.g.
62	Stu. Pz. IV, Brummbär	27·75	19 4	10 2	8 2	100	1 15-cm.
62	JgPz IV/70	25·8	19 9	10 6	6 1	80	1 7·5-cm., 1 m.g.
63	8·8-cm. PzJg Jagdpanther	44·78	22 7	10 9	8 11	80	1 8·8-cm., 1 m.g.
64	JgPz Elefant	66·93	22 4	11 3	9 9	200	1 8·8-cm.
65	JgPz VI, Jagdtiger	70·57	25 7	11 11	9 3	250	1 12·8-cm., 1 m.g.
66	7·5-cm. Pak auf Gw. 38(t) Marder III (Ausf. M)	10·80	14 9	7 1	7 11	25	1 7·5-cm., 1 m.g.
67	7·62-cm. Pak auf Gw. II, Ausf D.	11·50	15 3	7 7	6 8	30	1 7·62-cm.
68	8·8-cm. Pak auf Gw. III/IV, Nashorn	23·62	19 0	9 8	8 8	30	1 8·8-cm.
68	15-cm. PzfH auf Gw. III/IV, Hümmel	23·5	19 0	9 7	9 3	30	1 15-cm.
69	FlakpanzerWirbelwind	22·0	19 4	9 7	9 1	80	4 2-cm.
69	Flakpanzer Möbelwagen	25·0	19 4	9 7	10 2	80	1 3.7-cm.
	U.S.S.R.						
77	T-60	5·75	13 1	7 6	5 9	20	1 20-mm., 1 m.g.
73	T-34/76B	28·00	20 0	9 10	8 0	70	1 76·2 mm., 2 m.g
73	T-34/85	31·5	19 8	9 10	7 10	75	1 85-mm., 2 m.g.
74	KV-85	46·00	22 4	10 8	9 6	110	1 85-mm., 3 m.g.
75	JS-II	45·00	21 9	10 3	8 11	120	1 122-mm., 3 m.g.
77	SU-76	11·55	15 3	8 9	6 8	35	1 76·2-mm.
74	SU-85	29·00	19 5	9 10	8 1	75	1 85-mm.
76	JSU-122	45·5	22 4	10 1	8 2	90	1 122-mm., 1 m.g.
76	JSU-152	46·00	22 4	9 10	8 3	90	1 152-mm., 1 m.g.
	Sweden						
80	Strv. m/42	22·50	20 0	8 0	8 6	80	1 75-mm., 3 m.g.
80	Sav. m/43	12·00	15 1	8 3	7 7	25	1 10·5-cm.

Engine	b.h.p.	Speed m.p.h.	Range miles	Crew	Notes
ch	178	40	155	4	
ch	300	25	124	5	Length including gun 21 ft
ch	300	24	124	5	Length including gun 23 ft
ch	700	28	110	5	Length including gun 29 ft 1 in., turret max. 120-mm.
ch	700	24	62	5	Length including gun 27 ft, turret 110-mm.
ch	700	24	68	5	Length including gun 33 ft 8 in., turret 185-mm.
r-Benz	1200	12	118	6	Turret 240-mm.
ch	1200	24	130	6	700 b.h.p. engine fitted, turret 240-mm.
	150	25	111	4	Length including gun 20 ft 7 in.
ch	300	25	98	4	Length including gun 20 ft 2 in.
ch	300	24	124	5	
ch	300	25	124	4	Length including gun 28 ft 3 in.
ch	700	28	130	5	Length including gun 32 ft 4 in.
ch (×2)	640	12·5	93	6	Length including gun 26 ft 9 in.
ch	700	23	105	6	Length including gun 35 ft
	125	30	150	4	Length including gun 18 ft 8 in.
ch	140	34	93	4	Length including gun 18 ft 6 in.
ch	300	24	124	5	Length including gun 27 ft 8 in.
ch	300	24	124	6	Length including gun 21 ft 11 in.
ch	300	26	124	5	
ch	300	24	124	6	
2	70	27	380	2	
diesel	500	31	188	4	Length including gun 21 ft 7 in.
diesel	500	31	140	5	Length including gun 24 ft 7 in.
diesel	600	22	156	4	Length including gun 27 ft 10 in.
diesel	513	23	150	4	Length including gun 31 ft 6 in.
2 (×2)	140	48	280	4	
diesel	500	34	220	4	Length including gun 25 ft 9 in.
diesel	513	25	137	5	Length including gun 31 ft 4 in.
diesel	513	25	137	5	Length including gun 28 ft 9 in.
	380	29	—	4	
Vabis	140	27	—	4	

Ref. No.	Type	Weight tons	Length ft in.		Width ft in.		Height ft in.		Armour max. m.m.	Armament
8	*Japan* Armoured Personnel Carrier, ½-tracked, Type 1	7·00	20	0	6	11	6	7	8	—
	U.S.A.									
19	T.17E1 (Staghound)	13·70	18	0	8	10	7	9	32	1 37-mm., 2 m.g.
19	T.18E2 (Boarhound)	23·70	20	6	10	1	8	7	51	1 6-pr, 2 m.g.
20	M.8	7·80	16	5	8	4	7	4	19	1 37-mm., 1 m.g.
20	M.20	5·27	16	5	8	4	7	7	19	1 h.m.g.
18	Car, ½-track M.2A1	7·90	19	7	6	5	7	5	13	1 h.m.g., 1 m.g.
18	75-mm. G.M.C., M.3	9·40	20	5	7	1	8	3	16	1 75 mm.
	U.K., Canada, India and S. Africa									
39	Humber Mks III–IV	7·1	15	0	7	2	7	10	15	1 h.m.g., 1 m.g.
40	Daimler Mks I–II	7·5	13	0	8	0	7	4	16	1 2-pr, 1 m.g.
41	A.E.C. Mks II–III	12·7	17	10	8	10	8	10	30	1 6-pr, 1 m.g.
38	S.A. Mk IV	6·12	15	0	6	0	7	6	12	1 2-pr, 1 m.g.
38	S.A. Mk VI	11·00	18	8	7	3	—		30	1 2-pr, 1 m.g.
42	Scout Car, Humber	3·39	12	7	6	2	6	11	14	1 m.g.
43	Scout Car, Lynx II	4·00	12	1	6	1	5	10	30	1 m.g.
44	Light Recce Car, Humber Mk IIIA	3·50	14	4	6	2	7	1	10	1 a.t.r., 1 m.g.
44	Light Recce Car, Morris Mk II	3·70	13	3	6	8	6	2	14	1 a.t.r., 1 m.g.
43	Light Recce Car, Otter I	4·80	14	9	7	0	8	0	12	1 a.t.r., 1 m.g.
45	Carrier, I.P. Mk IIA	5·70	15	6	7	6	6	6	14	1 a.t.r., 1 m.g.
45	Carrier, I.P., A.O.V.	6·87	15	6	7	7	8	2	14	1 m.g.
47	Deacon	12·00	21	1	8	1	9	6	25	1 6-pr
47	Straussler S.P. 17-pr	8·00	26	5	9	5	5	4	25	1 17-pr
	Germany									
71	SdKfz 250/8	6·00	15	0	6	5	6	9	14·5	1 7·5-cm., 1 m.g.
71	SdKfz 250/9	6·00	15	0	6	5	6	11	14·5	1 2-cm., 1 m.g.
72	SdKfz 234/2 Puma	11·00	20	1	7	10	7	8	100	1 5-cm., 1 m.g.
72	SdKfz 234/3	10·50	20	1	7	10	7	0	30	1 7·5-cm., 1 m.g.
78	*U.S.S.R.* BA-64	2·4	12	0	5	0	6	3	10	1 m.g. or 1 h.m.g

Engine	b.h.p.	Speed m.p.h.	Range miles	Crew	Wheel arrangement	Notes
	134	31	190	15	½-track	
al Motors (two)	194	55	450	5	4 × 4	
al Motors (two)	250	50	250	5	8 × 8	
les	110	55	350	4	6 × 6	
les	110	55	350	6	6 × 6	
	147	45	200	10	½-track	
	147	45	220	5	½-track	
s	90	45	250	4	4 × 4	Mk IV has crew of 3 and 37-mm. gun instead of h.m.g.
er	95	50	205	3	4 × 4	Mk III: length 18 ft 5 in., 75-mm.
, diesel	158	41	250	4	4 × 4	
	95	50	200	3	4 × 4	
(two)	190	35	200	3	8 × 8	Width 8 ft 8 in. over spare wheels
er	87	60	200	2–3	4 × 4	
	95	57	200	2	4 × 4	
er	87	50	250	3	4 × 4	a.t.r. = 0·55 in. Boys anti-tank
	72	50	250	3	4 × 4	
al Motors	104	45	260	3	4 × 4	Typical armament given
	95	50		3–6	4 × 4	
	95	50		—	4 × 4	
, diesel	95	19		5	4 × 4	
rd	72	30	200	5	4 × 2	Third wheel also driven for gun traverse
ach	100	37	186	3	½-track	SdKfz = Sonderkraftfahrzeug (Special Motor Vehicle) —Prefix to ordnance numerical designations.
ach	100	37	186	3	½-track	
	220	53	375	4	8 × 8	
	220	53	375	5	8 × 8	
	50	31	375	2	4 × 4